TERI KARJALA

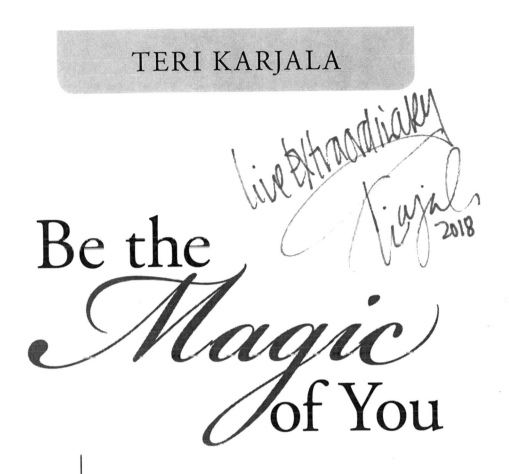

live Extraordinary
Tinjala
2018

Be the Magic of You

Tools to Transform Your Life!

BALBOA PRESS

A DIVISION OF HAY HOUSE

Balboa Press books may be ordered through booksellers or by contacting:

Balboa Press
A Division of Hay House
1663 Liberty Drive
Bloomington, IN 47403
www.balboapress.com
1 (877) 407-4847

Because of the dynamic nature of the Internet, any web addresses or links contained in this book may have changed since publication and may no longer be valid. The views expressed in this work are solely those of the author and do not necessarily reflect the views of the publisher, and the publisher hereby disclaims any responsibility for them.

The author of this book does not dispense medical advice or prescribe the use of any technique as a form of treatment for physical, emotional, or medical problems without the advice of a physician, either directly or indirectly. The intent of the author is only to offer information of a general nature to help you in your quest for emotional and spiritual well-being. In the event you use any of the information in this book for yourself, which is your constitutional right, the author and the publisher assume no responsibility for your actions.

Any people depicted in stock imagery provided by Thinkstock are models, and such images are being used for illustrative purposes only. Certain stock imagery © Thinkstock.

Print information available on the last page.

ISBN: 978-1-5043-8812-2 (sc)
ISBN: 978-1-5043-8814-6 (hc)
ISBN: 978-1-5043-8813-9 (e)

Library of Congress Control Number: 2017914620

Balboa Press rev. date: 02/05/2018

Be the Magic of You:
Tools to Transform Your Life!
Teri Karjala

ontents

Acknowledgments

I have been blessed with many amazing and dynamic people who have been right by my side on this journey. They have been my biggest supporters, mentors, and my "you can do it!" cheerleaders. I would not be where I am today without the love and support from my *rock star* team.

Steve Karjala: For being my rock, my best friend, and confidant. You support my larger than life dreams, accept my silly quirks, and truly are the love of my life. Thank you for riding this crazy roller coaster called life with me. I love you!

My mentors: Over the years, I have had many mentors that have shown up in my life and taken me under their wings. They have challenged me to play a bigger game and cheered me on in difficult times. Their continued support and encouragement has pushed me to create the business and life of my dreams!

My Mastermind Ladies: For being a part of the ups and downs, providing constructive feedback, holding me accountable, sharing in my successes, failures, and everything in between. It has been such a gift to be a part of a group that inspires me to live life to the fullest!

Kelly McGinnis: For continuing to ask, push, and support me in turning this book into reality. Thank you for being such a great friend in supporting my creation. I am so grateful!

Professionals: I have been so blessed to have brought into my life amazing individuals who have inspired me, taught me, and showed me the way. I thank everyone that has played a part in my life in supporting me and my dreams in laying the foundation of unlimited possibilities!

# Foreword

by Jack Canfield

Simply by realizing my dreams, maximizing my potential and achieving success, I have been given the unique opportunity to help countless others do the same. Inspiring people to change their lives. Motivating people to take action. Helping people build self-esteem and improve personal and professional performance. This is what I was born to do—*it is what I love to do*—and I stumbled upon most of it quite accidentally.

But there is a better way to discover your life's passion and achieve success than by stumbling upon it accidentally. It's just that most people, along this journey towards self-discovery, become, as Teri calls it, "stuck in the muck." They get boxed out by their fears, doubts, insecurities, limiting beliefs, excuses, and low self-esteem. In my many decades of experience guiding people towards greater success and fulfillment, I now know that almost all of these blocks come not from the outside, but from within. And this is the definition of self-sabotage.

So, how do you put a stop to these self-sabotaging thoughts and behaviors, get out of your own way, and become the author of your very own success story? That's what this book will teach you.

The same way that my own success now affords me the luxury of helping others, Teri Karjala's own achievement of emotional and professional prosperity makes her uniquely qualified to lead you through the process of becoming *unstuck*—of unlocking what Teri calls your "extraordinary" and transforming your life.

Coming from her extensive therapeutic background, Teri finds great joy in delivering hope, happiness and harmony to the lives of her clients. And now she brings that same expertise to you in this book. Teri's boundless energy, enthusiasm, intense magnetism and zest for life, make it impossible to not be inspired, empowered and left overflowing with excitement about the possibilities that await you on *your* journey towards greater happiness, fulfillment and success.

In this book, Teri shares the secrets of transformation—from eliminating the unconscious mental blocks that prevent you from chasing your dreams to expanding the boundaries of your comfort zone and taking inspired actions that ultimately lead you to living an extraordinarily magical life.

Teri is a truly extraordinary individual...and so are you. Go ahead, and let her help you unlock your mind, embrace your possibilities, and begin to experience *your* "extraordinary"—whatever it may be.

reface

The writing of this book has been a journey in itself. I distantly remember telling myself, "I'm never going to write a book" and then pondering the creation of a children's book. This type of book ... no. So why am I writing this book? Sometimes the universe has its own plan for us. When I say "the universe," I am referring to a place of unlimited possibilities, a magnificent place to live and be. Having said that, I also firmly believe that life is about finding our passion and living with a profound sense of joy.

I am professionally trained as a licensed professional counselor and marriage and family therapist. My training and my professional experiences have played integral parts in the writing of this book. I have known so much joy in getting to know people on a very personal and deep level. In this incredible way, I have been fortunate enough to be able to help support clients on their distinct life paths. No matter what the presenting issue was, I found my passion in helping others overcome and step into their greatness; to not only find happiness in their lives but to discover the magic within. To live life extraordinary is to embrace the gifts that we have been blessed with. On my path as a therapist and motivational speaker, I found that one of my greatest passions was sharing what

I have learned over the years about finding joy and really cultivating it into a lifestyle and way of being in the world. Thus this book became an idea, then a vision, and is now here, in your hands, a reality.

I have spent years working with children, adolescents, and adults who have been faced with incredible life challenges that have consumed their lives with anxiety, depression, fear, worry, and self-doubt. I wanted to find a way to do more than just tell my story. I wanted to give some concrete and effective tools to help shift people in a way that leaves lasting change in a way that transforms their realities. I truly desire more and more people to wake up to what they unknowingly hold inside and to allow that part to sparkle and shine to the world.

This book may not be for everyone. It is specifically for those who desire change, those with an open, searching mind, ready and willing to explore their full potential and all the possibilities that brings. It is for those who are aware that there is something grand and glorious about their life that they would like to tap into. If that is you, then *this book is for you!* If you are tempted to put this down, unsure about where you stand, chances are good that this book wound up in your hands here and right now for a reason, and despite your doubts, this book is for you too! After all, everything happens for a reason. Having this book in your hands is a sign of really amazing things to come!

I believe there are three types of people in the world: people on their way to greatness, people just getting out of the muck and waiting for what's next, and people who are still stuck and have been for years. This book is for all of you.

How I Got on This Path

I was so sick and tired of living within the realm of mediocrity I had created in my life. I was a solid seven, and some days more like a five. There were also many days early in my life when I struggled to get by with a three. That was not living extraordinary, not thriving—that was merely surviving. My journey started with me reading personal development books. One book would lead to another, and soon people would recommend the next one, and so one. The concepts of spiritually and the law of attraction were soon intertwined in my learning. I started to study and learn more about it, and then I started to implement my learning into my daily practice. I started seeing the results firsthand, and I couldn't help but start to believe in the magic. Things in my life started to shift with ease. I became obsessed with learning it and talking about it, and then I started teaching it, and now I'm writing about it.

We have all had those days when we somehow free ourselves from the doom and gloom we are in and experience an *extraordinary* day. You know the kind, when all the pieces seem to fall easily into place. Your thoughts are positive and support your current success story. You hit all the green lights on your way to work, you are complimented on how nice you look, someone treats you to a coffee, and you pick up the phone to speak to a friend you have been thinking about. It's *amazing!* I am here to challenge you to ponder the idea that you can have that day *every day.*

It started for me when I began looking at these two distinctly different states of being. I began wondering, How can I create more of that? What was I doing differently to create those kinds of results? What I discovered was that it really was up to me. In the beginning I noticed that my outside circumstances had a huge impact on how I felt, what I believed, and the way I acted. For example, in my business, when we were getting referrals I felt great! And when things happened negatively or when they didn't go my way, I felt horrible. I came to realize that these feelings were all a result of my perspective and expectations for what was taking place. What if I could shift that perspective to one that served me and didn't send me to an unpleasant place, a place where I was more likely to react out of fear and in turn receive more of what I didn't want? A place that was drenched in judgment, self-doubt, created out of a sense of lack. I chose to shift my thought processes and perceptions and create out of abundance.

So exactly how did I do that?

I was introduced to many, many different tools over the years. Many came from the traditional therapy world, and many more were discovered in the energy psychology domain. In the next few chapters we will explore the tools I have implemented in my life to create a more fulfilling and exciting life.

The bottom line is that my wish for you is simple. I wish that you see within yourself the gifts that you have been given, because once you unlock them you are going to feel the energy sparkle and come alive within you. Take the step into the unknown with courage, determination, and fierce gratitude. Then you can come to a place where you can wholeheartedly say "I *believe* in myself and I *know* that I *can* do this!" You will find that as you shine, others will be inspired and will look to you as the example that gives them the power to create their own phenomenal lives and step into the truth of knowing "I am enough." Let go of all the expectations, judgments, fears, worries, and the "muck" that is no longer serving you and unlock, embrace, and experience your extraordinary life. You are ready to rock the world!

For many, this will be new information; for those farther along their paths, this will act as a nice review and a reminder of who you are and where you came from. I include some really powerful tools throughout these pages that I have collected. I would love nothing more to share them with you so you, too, can reap benefits from them. I also love hearing the abundant success stories out there, so please contact me and tell me how you are living life extraordinary.

What if this is you? That would be pretty incredible, right? *What if it were possible?*

Psst … No one is stopping you from creating that reality! The only one stopping you is you.

I am here to say *you can do this!*

Let's start now, shall we?

I don't know about you, but I'm feeling pretty blessed right about now!

We were not born to be mediocre, average, or purposeless. No! We were created to live dynamic and extraordinary lives! Are you ready for this adventure?

When we look around, it might be easy to say this mediocre way of living is normal, but is that really what you desire? Be honest with yourself. Did you sign up for that? Maybe you signed up because you simply have not tasted the other. If that is true, I can't wait to meet you on the other side. I don't pretend to know everything, but what I can tell you is that I'm having a really amazing time going with the flow of life.

When you were in second grade and the teacher asked who or what you desired to be or do in life, did you respond "Just being mediocre"? Of course not. You were likely filled with passion, ideas, and excitement for what that could look like for you. If this was not your dream, why not start creating one now? Understand that you will not, I repeat *will not,* be able to please everyone. This is about you! Yes, you! So what if you were choosing for you?

Let's get it out right now. You are *not* selfish if you are taking care of your needs! You are the most important being on this planet at this very moment, and if you are not taking care of yourself, *no one else will.* Don't settle for mediocre because everyone else is doing so. You have choices here. You make thousands and thousands of choices every day. *You* get to choose how this all turns out. Wahoo!

Mediocrity settles in when we stop growing. According to dictionary.com, the word *mediocre* means "of ordinary or moderate quality." Most people are living a mediocre life without understanding why? If we dig deeper, it is based on belief systems placed there by someone other than themselves.

The time is now!

What does discovering your magic within mean?
It means waking up each morning and finding yourself filled with an unbelievable sense of gratitude. It is living life to the fullest, filling your life with an abundance of joy, happiness, and love all wrapped up with an incredible sense of purpose and playfulness.

Here's what that looks like:

- Owning your happiness. Take full responsibility for your life in every aspect.
- Eliminating your head trash. Transform the stories that are no longer serving you, and shift the way you think.
- Expanding outside your comfort zone. Discover comfort in the unknown.
- Creating your *rock star* team. Build a team that supports you in your journey of *big* dreams.

- Embracing gratitude. Find the gifts in even the darkest of times.
- Celebrating. Celebrate the blessings in your life every day.
- Taking inspired action. Take action by setting your dreams in motion and finding a daily practice that reinforces your path.

Some of the most extraordinary moments can come from very ordinary moments. Those are our defining moments in life. And it is up to us to determine how we respond to those events.

I hope that you come to know your true power.

I encourage you to come back and reread this book in your next stage in life; you will find that you have a new life perspective. Life energy is always changing, and when you have finished this book you, too, will have changed many, many, many times. Isn't that beautiful? I hope that if you have found value in these pages you share with others who may benefit in the same way that you have. Pay it forward. The more you give to others, the more you receive from others.

$\mathcal{I}$ntroduction

We were born to live life with purpose, passion, and playfulness. It is our birthright. Yet somewhere along the way we forget. We forget about the innate power inside of us. We dull our light ever so slightly to fit in, to be accepted, to simply belong. Yet most of us at some point in our lives are called to step into our greatness; we are absolutely terrified of what that could look like. We look to the scripts that have been playing in our heads, and there we find confirmation. "Play small. Don't rock the boat. You have never followed through with anything else in your life, so why start now? You can't do that. Who are you to be better than everyone else? You don't have the time. Don't kid yourself. People would not like you. You are too 'out there' for other people—they won't get you."

Yet, even in the face of this defeating, debilitating, and demoralizing self -talk, you have this deep, incredible knowing that you crave to understand. You begin to question the life you are living. And within the silence you know beyond a shadow of a doubt you were born for something so much more. You deserve to live an extraordinary life.

Most of us are dragged down into the muck, and we

can't live a life we are truly in love with. Over the years, I have discovered the power of personal development and tools that have helped me understand my passion and purpose in life. I have kept some, replaced some, and upgraded and tweaked others. I have been exposed to an endless number of modalities, and I have personally tested and included my absolute favorites in this book for you. These tools include Emotional Freedom Technique (EFT), Access Consciousness, and energy psychology, along with a few others.

It has been such an incredible journey. I would love to share some of my "secrets" with you. I am frequently asked, "How do you do it?" Within these pages you will find my secrets for staying out of the muck and living a life that I am truly in love with. I'm about to unveil all my trade secrets that are within all of us once we allow them to flow within us.

Let's create a foundation. Many people I speak to have a basic understanding of the law of attraction. Because I incorporate this concept in this book, I would like to make sure we are all on the same page moving forward. If you have heard this term before, you may be rolling your eyes, thinking, Yeah, right—that would never work for me. The fact is it does sound too good to be true. I have had many conversations with people who say, "Yes, I understand it, but it doesn't work for me." Does that sound familiar? Some people are easily frustrated, and come to the conclusion that it doesn't work for them. If it doesn't work for them, then it must not work for anyone else and therefore is not true. I get it, because I used to be that person too.

So am I saying if I change the way I think, voila, my life falls into place? Well, that does sound very magical, but in reality it does require more work on the individual's part. It really involves keeping the monkey mind balanced and eliminating our self-sabotaging tendencies. It takes work to uncover the blocks that hold us back on the cellular level of our beings. Some of the messages we picked up along our life's journey may have started before we really understood the language around us. We all have or have had these blocks; it's just a matter of how much we have worked on ourselves. The gift is that when we allow ourselves to be our priority, we grow exponentially. Part of living extraordinary includes implementing these concepts into your life to allow the magic you already hold within yourself to create your life intentionally.

People all around the world are incorporating the principles of the law of attraction into their lives, whether they know about it or even understand it. It's a universal law taking place in our lives *every day*. Whether you incorporate energy work, energy psychology, positive thinking, or spirituality, you are essentially applying resources within yourself to your work and life. This process not only benefits you but the world around you.

The law of attraction is basically the principle that like attracts like, which is another way of saying that whatever you focus on will expand. Thinking positive or negative thoughts to create positive or negative results is a simplified way to describe it, although many other factors are involved in incorporating this process into your life. When I was first introduced to this concept I right away began researching it. What I discovered was it could be brought back to quantum physics. Yes! It's science at its finest. Many people know the concept of the law of attraction from the popular film, *The Secret* (based on the book by the same name). *The Secret* is a great introduction to this concept; however, it does not address the millions of people who have head trash. *Head trash* is a term used to describe thoughts or beliefs that block an individual from achieving their goals in life. It would be wonderful and ideal if a person could quickly manifest just by focusing on positive thoughts related to their goal/target. However, it is much more complicated than that, and further reading, education, and practice is needed to fully implement this principle successfully.

Michael J Losier wrote a simple, yet powerful, book called *Law of Attraction*. What I love about this book is that it simply promotes understanding the laws of the universe and how we can apply them to our own lives. Losier states, "There is a physiological foundation for positive thinking and its effect in creating the law of attraction." He explains the science behind this theory, which is that all matter is made up of atoms. All energy vibrates at a certain frequency. Losier states that "vibrations exist in every living and nonliving thing in our world. There are only two vibrations, positive (+) and negative (-). Every emotion, thought, and every creation is made up of these vibrations, which are consistently giving off vibrations. The law of attraction is always responding to your vibrations in which you are giving off." Therefore, vibration attracts like vibration. For example, if you are turning on the radio to listen to a rock station, you expect to hear rock music. You do not turn to a rock station to hear country music or you will be disappointed. Simply put, the vibrations do not align. It is impossible for those two to align. Which is why when you are vibrating at a high frequency, things in your life tend to fall into place effortlessly. We all have the power to create the vibration we choose.

The law of attraction is really a law of nature that explains how atoms function in every living cell. I'll explain later why it doesn't seem to work for some people. Albert Einstein in the 1920s stated that all matter was made up of energy. Energy equals positive or negative charges. Everything is made up of energy. If I placed my bracelet under a high-powered microscope, we would see atoms moving, therefore energy. If I were to do this to any object, I would have the same result. Humans are no different; we are energy beings in constant motion. We tend to take this fact for granted living in our day-to-day lives.

The law of attraction is not a law that works for some of us and not the rest. It is actually operating at all times, whether we believe in it or not. I get a kick out of observing people who have no idea of this concept but are completely in the flow of life, using it to their full advantage. Some people are truly gifted at going through life with less of the head trash that gets in the way, blocking our flow.

I get excited when looking at the bigger picture and how we impact others and our community on a collective-consciousness level. When we give ourselves permission to take the step into our amazingness, it has a direct impact on others doing the same, therefore creating a magical domino effect. Are you ready to play?

In the many talks that I give, I almost always encounter someone in disagreement with the law of attraction. This is understandable, and, quite frankly, I was one of those people—until I started to learn more about this principle and how it works.

A great explanation of the scientific basis for the law of

attraction is given by Dr. Joe Dispenza in his book *Evolve Your Brain*. Dr. Dispenza describes how biology, physiology, and quantum mechanics all play very intricate and real roles in this process. *Evolve Your Brain* is a worthwhile read for anyone with doubts about the scientific validity of the law of attraction and how the law works.

My own personal experience has become proof enough for me. I have found that implementing this principle through the tools I outline in this book has allowed me to invite more ease into all areas of my life. I have seen just how easily things can fall into place. My business has become much more successful and continues to grow with less and less physical effort on my part. In short, life has become much more stress-free in many ways, which frees up energy to spend time on what is most important to me: my family.

I came across a congratulatory card I wrote to myself more than seven years ago. I sent it to myself in the mail and just kept it. I discovered it sitting in an old work bag, and when I read it, it took me back to that moment it was created. I had forgotten all about the card. To my surprise, I had achieved all the desires I'd written down—every single one. This a fun exercise. Send yourself a card expressing congratulations for the successful achievement of certain goals/targets you have in mind. I recommend thinking *big*!

What we create within is mirrored outside
of us. That is the law of the universe.
—Shakti Gawain

hapter 1

Words Have Power

Words have the power to both destroy and heal.
When words are both true and kind,
they can change our world.
Buddha

Here's what I've learned in discovering the magic within: the power of words is undeniable. I thought I knew the answers to life until I become aware of the predictability of my life. I lived daily with feelings I thought were deemed normal by society. The truth is, I was just existing in what seemed to be a mundane world. Routine had become comfortable for me and ultimately left my life stagnant. I was simply living an ordinary life. My passion and zest for life had been lost. One day I started challenging this state and became curious, asking myself, "What else is out there?"

Have you ever been so beaten down by life that you were left feeling completely alone, afraid, and, worst of all, hopeless? As if you were hollow inside. Feeling numb, confused, and completely invisible? Knowing that you are one person to the core, but being told something so very different? Hard enough as an adult, but imagine as a young child?

Let me take you on a journey. Imagine for a moment a young, innocent, shy, little girl who grew up in a small town, naive and unaware of the possibilities of life beyond her front door. She was constantly told that she just wasn't enough and had begun to see the world through an obscured and cloudy lens. Words, seemingly harmless at first, were carelessly and continuously planted. The seeds of discouragement, "You are stupid," "You're never going to be anything." "You are a failure," "What's wrong with you?" were sown.

These words grew to become a part of her life and soon a part of her identity. Words have power. These words became her truth, filling her soul with self-doubt, shame, sadness, and self-hate. She began to shrink and became very small in the world. One day she cried out. This is not my life!

This story was my story. You see, I lived the lies from someone else's story. It was so subtle that I didn't even know it was happening until it was too late. I had swallowed the lies piece by piece. I was left broken and constantly felt the need to prove myself. You see, if you are told something once, so what. Told twice…hmmm maybe something to this. Told again and again and again… those words became my truth. I did what most people do. I locked it in. My brain did its job and found the evidence to support every single lie until I believed it too.

But deep down- I didn't want to believe it.

But then there it was the fuel. The fuel that I needed to prove those words wrong, but more importantly I wanted to discover who I really was, my authentic self. Some days were harder than others, I wanted to give up and give in to the story.

But I made a choice.

At a point, when part of me wanted so desperately to end it all, I chose to get up and fight. To fight for it all. I did the things that I'm asking you to do today. I discovered the magic within. I chose to shine.

Words have power. I had choices. I could have easily said that he was right and given in, but I chose to change my thinking and create something different. It is difficult to say with absolute certainty what kept me from choosing the other fate: doom, despair, rejection. At times I wonder where intuition fits in. Somewhere within me, I knew that I was going to fight his influence. Some may say it was my age, my personality, or maybe just plain old courage. Regardless of why it occurred, I gave birth to the notion that I would never give up or give in. This didn't occur without occasional bouts of self-doubt in which I wondered if those negative words that he'd so carelessly thrown at me might somehow be true. Yet I found myself surrounding myself with people who supported me and relayed a much different message. The message came in many forms: "You *can* do it!" "You inspire me." "You will accomplish amazing things in your life," to name a few. *Words have power.*

I would like to tell you that this was the only time in my life I struggled with self-doubt and overcoming deep emotional wounds, but that, of course, would be a lie. I am sure that I am not alone in this either. We all have something to overcome, a hurdle to vault over. The challenge is to take what life gives you and choose to

3

turn it into something else, something magical, to give power to what really matters, to the words that inspire, motivate, and bring life into your spirit.

Words affect the messages that we tell ourselves and others, and eventually they become the foundation of the stories that dominate and steer our paths. Yet, looking back, I can appreciate the gifts that the messages this person of influence unknowingly gave me: a profound drive and motivation that still fuels me today.

I get to choose the messages I tell myself—words have power. We are not able to change the details of the past, but we can choose how we step forward in the present.

> The word is not just a sound or a written symbol.
> The word is a force, it is the power you have
> to express and communicate, to think,
> and thereby to create the events of your life.
> —Don Miguel Ruiz

Jack Canfield, in his book *The Success Principles: How to Get from Where You Are to Where You Want to Be,* provides a beautiful summary of just how important our words are. "If I express love and acceptance to you, you will experience love for me. If I express judgment and contempt for you, you will judge me back. If I express gratitude and appreciation for you, you will express gratitude and appreciation back to me. If I express words of hatred toward you, you will most likely hate me back."

What if we shifted our perspectives to this boomerang concept—what I put out there comes back to me? What if more and more people got it that this *is* how the world works. Can you imagine the beauty that we would create? *Wow!* That gives me the shivers.

Going back to the energy of our world, *everything* that we create has and is made up of energy. Therefore, even the words we speak to ourselves and to others have energy. That energy, in return, has a direct impact on us and others. In 1994, a Japanese scientist named Dr. Masura Emoto began experimenting with water and the power of words. He used various methods, speaking words, showing pictures, playing music, and praying to the water. After freezing the water and observing the molecules under a high-powered microscope, he discovered that the water molecules changed shapes, creating crystal formations. Positive messages and expressions resulted in beautiful crystals, while negative messages and expressions created unpleasant and malformed ones. Now, just think. If our bodies are made up of 90 percent water, what is the impact that these messages can have on our bodies at the cellular level?

Here are a few of the images from his research:

Positive
Love and gratitude   Thank you

Negative

Heavy metal music   You make me sick, I will kill you

**Pictures: Permission for use given by Dr. Masaru Emoto

You can view his entire collection of research in his books, including *Messages from Water* and *The Hidden Messages in Water*. His work was also highlighted in the award-winning film *What the Bleep Do We Know?*

I discovered that Dr. Emoto also created a rice experiment with a similar premise but without the use of a high-powered microscope. Once I learned about this, I felt compelled to re-create the experiment in my very own home. What I loved about it was that I was able to get kids involved in the process and educate them on the importance of the words that we speak to others. The results: the positive statement "you are amazing" allowed the first jar of rice to remain looking fresh, whereas in the jar where we communicated the negative message "you are stupid," the rice spoiled and turned dark brown. I also choose to keep one jar as the "control" in which I did nothing to it. This was really fascinating. For the first few months it remained clear but over the course of my experience it too began to take on the same qualities of the negative jar." I realize that my home is not a sterile laboratory, but I could not help but notice the startling difference between the two jars of rice. This was an excellent way to demonstrate the power of words in a visual and concrete way. *Words have power.*

Negative words keep us stuck in the muck and prevent us from moving forward toward our full potential. Positive words allow us to become the people we were born to be. They allow energy to flow within us, propelling us forward toward our ever-expanding selves.

Here are the end results after a year and a half of repeating the words "you are stupid" and "you are amazing."

Rice experiment

The way in which we view the world, through a lens of either positivity or negativity, is a powerful force. Please understand that I am not saying that there is no value or purpose in negativity, because there is. All emotions serve an incredible purpose to help us to navigate our world based on that information.

Now let's do a quick exercise to see where you stand, based on your viewpoint.

On a scale of one to ten—with one equaling feeling stuck in the muck, lifeless, and hopeless, and ten equaling loving life, feeling amazing, and having energy and excitement about where your next adventure will take you— where do you rate yourself, just for today? Where do you rate yourself on your overall life? Be honest with yourself.

I ask this question a lot, and I typically get a vast range, but most often between three and seven. I've asked hundreds of people, and only four people rated themselves as a ten.

6, 3, 3, 4, 6, 3, 2, 7, 3, 4, 5, 4, 5, 1, 3, 6, 5, 4, 5, 6, 5, 3, 4, 3, 4, 5, 4, 5, 6, 2, 8, 4, 5, 5, 7, 6, 3, 7, 4, 3, 5, 4, 6, 7, 5, 4...

What is happening here?

Why settle for ordinary when we can create anything—including being extraordinary? (I get so excited just saying that!)

When you look at a newborn baby, what would rate him/her? A ten, of course. If you have children, or if not, what would you rate children? Ten, of course. How about teenagers? I know what you are thinking: Heck *no*—they are not a ten." But yes, they too are a ten! Now wouldn't that same line of reasoning apply to you as well? Of course! You are a ten too—*every day!* We are *all* born as pure amazing beings, here to discover and fulfill our life purpose. The challenge lies when we confuse the difference between our identity and our behavior. Our identity is a ten every day. However, the choices we make with our behavior change. For example, when I make a mistake, I might rate my behavior as an eight, but that still does not change my identity as a being here on earth, which is always a ten! Just knowing that and implementing this concept had an incredible impact on my life. How many of you just thought, Yes! You are right I am a ten! You might have given yourself a pat on the back and looked around to see if anyone saw you ... It's okay, go ahead. After all, *you rock,* my friend! This is us, our true identity. Please understand that the ratings of our behaviors and feelings change from moment to moment, but who we truly are *never* drops below a ten!

When we have a rough day and we make a mistake, our behavior rating might change to a seven or an eight, but we still remain a ten! Wahoo! Don't you already feel better about yourself? And we haven't even gotten to the fun stuff yet!

I have found that most people are pretty content with where they are in their lives, mostly because they have never given themselves permission to look outside to what else is possible for them. So many have been laughed at or told that their dreams are just not realistic. Poof, just like that their dream ... died. Their lives became stories of complacency. Many people come into my office in this exact state, feeling completely hopeless.

Why are we giving ourselves permission to live at this standard? What messages have we been exposed to that do not allow us to live our highest potential. I was told I couldn't do things so many times I once questioned if it was true. Never give up on your dreams because someone else is afraid of their own.

... 5, 6, 3, 3, 4, 6, 3, 2, 7, 3, 4, 5, 4, 5, 4, 3, 6 ...

Chapter 2

Own Your Happiness

You must take personal responsibility. You cannot
change the circumstances, the seasons, or the wind,
but you can change yourself.
—Jim Rohn

To own the very essence of our being is to step into our
authentic selves fully and with abandon. It is letting go
of who we think we "should" be and "could have" been,
as well as what others have told us about ourselves. Only
by releasing this do we give ourselves the freedom to
truly discover who we are and to fall in love with every
little bit of ourselves. It means taking responsibility for our
consciousness and our life on a conscious level, to be the
entirety of ourselves all the time. To be authentic is to be
vulnerable, to trust in ourselves when no one else does,
to not have it all figured
out and still know that it
will all be okay. It means
to stand with courage
and strength in the most
challenging of times
and at the end of the
day to know you did
your best. To own your

> **"**
> To own your own
> happiness you must be
> willing to free yourself from
> the past and the stories that
> no longer serve you. **"**

own happiness you must be willing to free yourself from the past and the stories that no longer serve you.

It is said that we make about thirty-five hundred choices a *day*. That is a ton of choices. Think about it. We choose to get up with our alarm clock or not; to shower or not; to brush our hair or not. You get the picture. We probably burn through two thousand choices just getting ready in the morning. We make a lot of choices throughout the day, and therefore we get to choose how we show up, how we act, and how we respond to the situations in our lives. These are repetitive patterns that have been reinforced time and time again. What if we chose something completely different?

The choices we make are ultimately responsible for the life we live. No one else is in our shoes, making those choices. As human beings, we all share one entitlement: to be *happy*. Taking inventory of what I perceived to be holding me back was enormously beneficial during this process. For me, that also meant setting boundaries with people who did not share my passion for my vision. This included placing limits on other people's requests for my time and energy. When we blame others for situations in our lives, we are effectively giving our power away. When we are able to take responsibility for our lives as they stand, we take back our power and control over those circumstances.

The day I realized I was the only one responsible for my own happiness, shifts started happening. The biggest shift became knowing within my heart that I could do this. Confidence began to take over as I developed a plan to make my dreams reality. My feelings vacillated between fear and excitement. But change had begun. It was time for me to take responsibility for my own happiness. At that moment, I stopped playing the victim and stopped hoping that everyone else around me would change.

I asked myself these questions:

- Am I truly happy?
- Am I going to continue down this path with the same results?
- What can I do to change this?

Is it time for change? Yes.

That's the moment when life as I knew it changed forever. The leap of faith …

What if we give up everything that keeps us from owning our own happiness, such as the excuses we have created, complaining, blaming others, judgments, expectations, justifications, and the "it's not my fault" syndrome. All of these keep us playing small in the game of life.

What would that be like?

We are responsible. Whenever we allow others to dictate our happiness, it's over. We give up our power and become powerless. Remember: we get to choose how we show up, how we respond and react to any given situation. Owning your life is about loving yourself.

E+R=O

The equation E+R=O, taught to me by Jack Canfield, breaks this concept of responsibility down in an easy-to-understand format. E=Event + R=Response equals O=Outcome. You are creating your experiences, your successes, your failures, your relationships, your health, your wealth, etc., through what you think, feel, and believe and how you act. You have control over these things. Every outcome you experience in this life is a direct result of how you reacted or responsed to the event. The joy in all of this is that we are in control of our actions; therefore, if we are not happy with the result we can always change our response. We can continue to change our response until we get the outcome we desire. Take a minute to think about recent situations in your life. Put them into this equation. Does that provide some insight on how the outcome came about for you? If it wasn't the outcome you desired, how could you have shown up differently to create a different reality?

I give you permission to be all that you truly are ... all of the time. No more shrinking so you can fit within the reality you have created for yourself. You were made to be extraordinary! So break out of that confining box, break free of that story. You are here for great and glorious adventures. Let's give you permission to own this moment and how you show up. We get to make choices every day, so choose from your heart to love and accept you *as you are.*

There are tools to help you begin to own your happiness, and I've assembled them for you below. Think of this section as your very own toolbox. You can use the tools at different times so you're always on track.

Own Your Happiness Toolbox

Self-Sabotage Exercise: This is one of my favorite exercises over the years, and I use it every day. There are two prerequisites for this tool. 1) No stink eye when I describe this ... no "What?" (and no skipping this section—*don't do that!* This is great stuff!) 2) Try it for one week, at least ten times a day, before you judge it. I was taught this exercise, designed to keep people out of self-sabotaging tendencies, by an energy coach. When we are living in the unconscious mindset and allowing our past to control our lives, we are not living to our fullest potential. We sabotage our success on every level. So here is an exercise to help support us in living more consciously. https://vimeo.com/talkingwithteri/whatiseft

Step 1. Tap the side of your hand, also known as the karate chop point, fifteen times. (See Appendix D.)

Step 2. Bring your right hand to your collarbone and rub with thumb and first two fingers; place your left index finger in your belly button just for a few seconds.

Step 3. Reverse hands. Bring your left hand to your collarbone and rub with thumb and first two fingers; place your right index finger in your belly button just for a few seconds.

Step 4. Tap under your nose fifty times.

Step 5. Tap under your lower lip fifty times.

I encourage people to do two or three rounds until you notice the shift that allows you to know that you are out of self-sabotage. I do these back to back until I notice the energy shift. The energy shift might be different for each person. I yawn. Others people have reported feeling lighter and their voice becomes clearer; they sigh and feel calmer. Some people burp! All of these responses are considered normal; they are the body's way of releasing.

I recommend doing this exercise about ten times a day. During times of transitions or change, I do more, sometimes twenty or more rounds. The reason for the increase is that, if you are anything like me, changes in our lives can easily take us back to our "maybe not so great" default mode that we were programmed for.

Access Consciousness: One of the techniques I was exposed to and quickly took a liking to was Access Consciousness, founded by Dr. Gary Douglas. It offers "pragmatic tools to change things in your life that you haven't been able to change until now." It provides ways to become the conscious being that you are here to be. What I like about this simple yet profound process is that it allows us to ask questions to impact our energy, space, and consciousness. In other words, it helps to keep the energy flow open, if you will. In doing so, we allow ourselves to become more of our extraordinary selves without the limitations that hold us back. Too often we make decisions, place judgments, jump to conclusions— all the while, we are cutting ourselves off from the universal energy that connects and is a part of everything and everyone. By asking questions we open ourselves to the greater possibilities of the universe. It allows us to come to a place of being connected with the universe and being in the flow.

To start, write down one or two of these on a sticky note and start to implement them into your day. You will be amazed at how you will start shifting your world. For fun, I also like to use these while sitting in traffic, waiting in line, and anytime I go anyplace. They just become part of what I am creating in my everyday life.

"What else is possible?"

Access Consciousness energy questions:

- Who am I today? What great and grand and glorious adventures am I going to have and receive today?
- No matter what I step into, what would it be like to perceive, know, be, and receive all of me without judgment, perfect of not?
- What contribution can I be and receive today? (Say three times.)
- What can I do to create a different reality?
- What can I do to change this?
- What can I create today to create and generate in my life/business?
- What would I change if I knew the universe was on my side?
- How does it get any better than this? (Use when you perceive something as negative or positive.)
- What's right about this situation that I'm not getting?
- What would it take to change this?
- All of life comes to me with ease, joy, and glory.

The second part of Access Consciousness that I love is the clearing statement. It is designed to bring up the energies of any limitation and clear them. Fortunately, you do not have to understand it for it to work. It is designed to bypass your logical mind and access your insane mind, which is where the answers to the life you are creating live. It helps to give you more awareness and more ability to function from consciousness. You can say this for anything that blocks you from living your life fully. For example, for anything that does not allow (blank) in your life, ask, "Are you willing to revoke, recant, destroy, and uncreate all of that?"

If the answer is yes, follow it by saying this clearing statement: "Right and wrong, good and bad, POC and POD, all nine, shorts, boys and beyonds." (See Appendix A for a definition.)

Here's an example of how you set it up. Say this to yourself, "For anything that does not allow me to create more joy in my life, am I willing to revoke, recant, destroy, and uncreate all of that? Yes! Right and wrong, good and bad, POC and POD, all nine, shorts, boys and beyonds."

The magic of this tool is that you can use it on *anything*! To discover more about this technique, visit www.accessconsciousness.com.

Emotional Freedom Technique (EFT)
Emotional Freedom Technique entered my life more than fourteen years ago, and I have been using it ever since. Emotional Freedom Technique is best described as an emotional version of acupuncture that stimulates the various meridian points located on our bodies with a tapping motion. This technique is designed to help balance the energy system in our body. It has been used for array of emotional issues, including but not limited to: stress, anxiety, fears, phobias, attracting abundance, trauma, self-esteem, releasing blocks, shifting thoughts, and even sports performance. Albert Einstein's theory of relativity further demonstrates why EFT is so effective. "All matter is made up of energy," which is made up of positive and negative charges. The foundation of EFT is based on the discovery statement "The cause of all negative emotions is a disruption in the body's energy system."

The founder of EFT was committed to finding a universal

tool that anyone could master and created this easy to follow, simple to do one-minute technique. The process is comprised of four basic ingredients: setup, sequence, nine gamut, and the repeating sequential.

Studies have shown that EFT can quickly lower or eliminate distress and limit the effect of memories on an individual, which can often promote quicker relief from symptoms. The cells of your body unconsciously hold onto the upsetting thought or memory that impacts your perceptions and your worldview. The tapping helps to counter these negative signals and help break up old chemical patterns to neutralize them and reduce the physiology connected to the event. Learn more at www.eftuniverse.com

As you learn this new tool, turn to Appendix B in the back of this book for a more in-depth set of directions for how to do EFT, including step-by-step instructions.

EFT Script: Own Your Happiness
https://vimeo.com/talkingwithteri/happiness

For best results, tune into a particular negative thought or story that has been blocking you and your success as you go through the sequences provided as a guide for you.

To start, rate yourself on a scale from zero to ten, ten equaling worst; zero equaling best. Where do you rate yourself on truly owning your happiness?

Tap on the karate chop point while saying the following:

- Even though I'm not sure I'm ready to really own my own happiness because that would mean me being happy, I deeply and completely love and accept myself.
- Even though I'm not deserving of my own happiness, I deeply and completely love and accept myself.
- Even though I'm afraid of stepping into my own happiness, I deeply and completely love and accept myself.

Round 1 (Negative Reminder phrases)

Key:
Key:

H: Even though I have been telling myself a really great story all of these years
EB: I'm not sure that I'm ready to give up that story.
SE: What if I could be happy, truly happy?
UE: What if life could be easy?
UN: I'm not sure about that. I've been told it has to be difficult.

H=Head
EB=Eyebrow
SE=Side of eye
UE=Under eye
UN=Under nose
CH=Chin
CB=Collarbone
UA=Under arm

CH: I choose to know that I am open to receiving all of the possibilities in my life.

CB: I allow myself to be open to me *loving* my life!

UA: I am responsible for creating my happiness, and I choose to start now!

Round 2 (Positive phrases)

**Repeat as needed.

H: I am allowing happiness, joy, and glory to flow into my life with ease.

EB: I choose to grateful for *all* that I am and *all* that I have.

SE: I am allowing an abundance of joy to flow into my life.

UE: I deserve to be happy and show up as my magnificent self.

UN: I trust in this process of allowing incredible adventures to show up in my life.

CH: Happiness fills me.

CB: I am choosing to create my own happiness. I love my life.

UA: I am blessed and filled with gratitude.

Continue going through this sequence until you reach zero.

So what are you waiting for? Here is your opportunity to create and live the life of your dreams!

Chapter 3

Get Yourself Out of Your Way

Whether you think you can or you
think you can't, you're right.
—Henry Ford

What is the "muck?"

Over the years, I have often spoken about the concept of living in the muck. We live in a world that makes it easy to live trapped in this state of mind. The muck is more than just the negative self-talk we tell ourselves. It is a state of being that disempowers us, fills us with self-doubt, self-hate, worry, fear, mediocrity, and an overall feeling of hopelessness from knowing that we are not living our lives to our full potential. I am referring to a moment in your life when you are beating yourself up for one thing or another, consumed with apprehension and not sure where you are going or if you have the energy to get there. It is the place where we are consumed by fear, worry, and self-doubt, feeling insecure, out of sync, and stripped from your ability to create and generate the great stuff in life. It often is a time that everything seems forced or just plain difficult. We have all been here at one time or another, and what we tell ourselves traps us there even longer. (See Fig. 1)

At what point did you stop living your amazing life based on someone else's story, rejection, fear, judgment, inadequacy, or failure to see us for *all* of us? What would it take for us to really show up? I mean to really show up?

I have been asked if I ever get angry, if I ever have a bad day. The answer is yes, but I choose to move quickly out of that state. I remember in the beginning it was very much a different story. Whether your muck lasts a day, a week, a month, or even longer, it is possible to shift it. Doing this work on myself has allowed me to shift out of the muck from long periods of time to just a few minutes. And yes, you too are in control of this amazing power. The first step is recognizing the difference when you are in the muck from when you are living extraordinary! In that transition we can start shifting the intensity and frequency. The more you practice the tools I outline in this book, the more you will find yourself shifting to a place where ease, joy, and glory live within.

Many circumstances and situations contribute to this state of mind. I like to start helping people by having them eliminate the negativity in all aspects of their lives. It only takes a few minutes of listening, watching, or witnessing the news to find ourselves deep in this disheartening place. The media constantly fills the page, airwaves, and

> Muck
>
> A state of being that disempowers and fills us with self-doubt, self-hate, worry, fear, mediocrity, and an overall feeling of hopelessness from knowing that we are not living our lives to our fully potential.

screen with news of war, acts of violence, and other fear-inducing stories. As technology has evolved, the media has even more of a presence within our lives, through our phones, tablets, computers, radios, and televisions. We literally have access to the muck every waking minute of our lives. I wish positive things happening in the world had a place in what we call the news. I wonder what things would shift as a result. What would people aspire to if they knew their success story would be highlighted? What messages would we send out if we broadcast uplifting, inspiring, and life-changing stories? What are we afraid of? Why must we continue to contribute to people's fears and reinforce all the bad in the world? If we really look at it, there are billions of more positive things happening in the world. I full-heartedly believe that our media has a profound and powerful role in what we think, feel, and experience and has a direct impact on our lives. What if we took the media challenge and chose to fill our lives with people, places, and things that inspire, empower, and transform our lives? Wouldn't that be amazing? It is easy for me to point my finger at the media at large, but we know that when we point our finger we have three more fingers pointing back at us. Because the truth of the matter is *it is our choice.* We choose to allow this into our reality. We all have the ability to turn off the news and fill that hour with what we value (i.e., family, friends, education, etc.), but do we? Let's face it. Our brains are hardwired to perceive threats, and in many ways our brains are designed to feed off it. Let's give our brains a break for once.

Because so much of our muck comes through the media, I challenge you to a media challenge. Simply reduce or eliminate the news for a period of time, a few days to a few months. I want you to journal your experience and see what you notice as a result. After that period, feel free to choose what you do next. Did you notice any shifts in your perspective of the world? Did you feel like you missed out on anything? The next part of this challenge is to fill in that time with something inspiring, motivating, and enriching to you. Then sit back and observe what happens within you. Exciting things are waiting for you to show up for them!

I'm so excited for you! I'm convinced that you will automatically drop ten pounds of negatively from your life, just like that!

Our lives are also filled with the day-to-day stories from the past, present, and even the future that we tell ourselves. As discussed in Chapter 1, *words have power*. What are the words we tell ourselves? Does the tape recorder that plays in the background in your mind serve to propel you forward or is it sabotaging your success? It's important to look at words such as *don't, never,* and *no*. I have found that as people are able to let go and transition themselves away from these words, they open themselves up to much, much, more. Michael J. Loiser explains that when we use these words we are simply giving attention and focus to the very things we don't desire. Based on the law of attraction, where we place our focus is what we generate. By simply shifting these words, we place ourselves on a path of asking and expecting our true desires in life.

What if, in a moment of being stuck in the muck, you choose to shift your perspective? What if getting stuck in the muck allows you to become consciously aware of the difference between that feeling and the feeling of living extraordinary? What if being there has brought you more gifts than you could even imagine?

I remember that I wished for a different life for the longest time. I wished for something more, but I found myself holding onto the anger of the situation. Now I am able to realize that I am stronger for having gone through it. We *all* have stuff. It may come in a different package, but we all have our stories that make each of our lives special and truly unique. In this place of awareness, you get to choose something different, something even better! Yay! The power *is* yours!

I know what you are thinking: "But Teri, I have tried to take ownership of my life, and it still turns out bad." Or "That sure sounds great, but the last time I tried to change the situation in my life I found myself in a worse place than when I started, and I'm not going to try that again." I get it! There is an answer. Let's read on.

I was once told by a mentor that you have to be in that crappy place in order to learn what is required to get you out of that place. That is the place where lasting transformation can occur. Discovering how to "have it" and "lose it" and have it again, allowing me to maintain the flow for longer and longer periods of time, was a pivotal moment in my own life.

How are we re-creating the muck in our lives?

> Your beliefs become your thoughts.
> Your thoughts become your words.
> Your words become your actions.
> Your actions become your habits.
> Your habits become your values.
> Your values become your destiny.
> —Mahatma Gandhi

When we think about it, there is a conscious or unconscious payoff to us that gets in our way of achieving our desires. Think about the areas in your life where you have felt blocked or limited in some way. Now, take a moment for yourself and answer the following question.

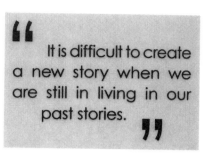

It is difficult to create a new story when we are still in living in our past stories.

What is the *value* in keeping yourself in your own way?

_____

_____

_____

_____

_____

_____

_____

_____

_____

_____

_____

_____

_____

_____

_____

As we discussed in the previous chapter, let's implement the clearing statement from Access Consciouness here. Now, anything that, that is times a billion gazillion ... Are you willing to revoke, recant, destroy, and uncreate all of that? Say, "Yes!"

Right and Wrong, Good and Bad, POC and POD, All Nine, Shorts, Boys and Beyonds.

Get yourself out of the way!

Where does our head trash come from? Head trash is picked up along our life path. Some is intentionally passed on, and some is unintentionally passed on. These are messages you picked up from your family of origin, friends, teachers or professors, colleagues, neighbors, etc. Each has their own head trash that governs how they interact with the world around them. The messages get passed down from one to another, and so on and so forth. Dr. Joe Dispenza said, "A highly charged experience in our external reality will impress itself upon the circuitry of the brain and emotionally brand the body. As a result, the brain and body live in the past, and the event alters our state of being, as well as our perception of reality. We are no longer the same personality." These beliefs and perceptions then become part of the state of being in which we currently live.

According to the National Science Foundation, we have anywhere from twelve thousand to fifty thousand thoughts a day. Some estimates run as high as sixty thousand a day (one thought every second). In Dr. Dispenza's book *You Are the Placebo*, he states that 90 percent of our thoughts are ones we had the day before, therefore replicating the same choices, behaviors, and experiences as the day before. These thought patterns become ingrained and reinforced, creating a circuitry of the same.

It is reported that 90 percent of who we are is subconscious or unconscious, which means your conscious mind consists of the remaining 10 percent. Let's take the example of the iceberg (see iceberg diagram). We know that 10 percent of the iceberg is visual to the eye; however, the majority of the mass of the iceberg is located below the water surface. This is very similar to our mind. Which do you suppose is the stronger of the two? You got it—the subconscious and unconscious part of our mind. It truly dominates the rest of mind, so the 90 percent is working against the other 10 percent. The challenge for most people is shifting to a positive mindset when they are still being bombarded with the 90 percent negative subconscious mind that has been programmed for the past thirty years. It is difficult to create a new story when we are still in living in our past stories.

According to Dr. Dispenza, "The brain processes four hundred billion bits of information a second. But we are *only* aware of two thousand of them." Psychological researchers state that 80 percent of those thoughts are negative. A positive mental attitude plays a huge part in allowing us to reach our targets, as well as our overall happiness. Which one would you say is stronger, the two thousand conscious thoughts or the forty-eight thousand negative thoughts? These thoughts happen to be the information that we base our choices on. Our thoughts are hugely responsible for the choices we make each and every day. When people tell me law of attraction does not work for them, that is why.

ICEBERG

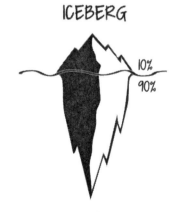

Negativity contributes to our level of stress because negativity is responsible for releasing stress chemicals in the body. Anyone stressed knows that negativity contributes to that stress. Stress has huge implications for our bodies, including our overall health. It has been said that 95 percent of all major medical conditions can be traced back to stress. The Center for Disease Control reports a direct link between stress and six of the leading causes of death, including heart disease, cancer, lung ailments, accidents, cirrhosis of the liver, and suicide.

Negative events have a bigger impact on our brain because they are associated with a level of perceived threat. Try this: think back to the past week or so. What challenging or negative thing happened to you or was said to you? Now, what really amazing or positive happened to you or was said to you? Which one was easier to retrieve and recall? If you are like most people, the negative experience was probably easier to recall, as it has more charge to it. It is easy to get stuck in the negative cycle that has significant power over us. That is why it is even more important to constantly counteract it to deactivate it, if you will, giving it less potency over us. Most of the time negativity becomes so ingrained you may not even notice it.

Every function that we perform consciously, or even unconsciously, is done by some part of the brain. An important part of the brain is the reticular activation system (RAS), which holds significant influence over human cognition.

What Is the RAS?
The reticular activation system (RAS) is a concept introduced by Tony Robbins in *Awaken the Giant Within*.

The RAS is an automatic system that brings important information to our conscious awareness. This part of the subconscious mind acts as a filter applied to the data that we process every second of our lives. This area in our brain helps to determine what information we see or hear and what we don't see or hear. It also pulls our attention to whatever is most intriguing to us at that moment.

This area in the brain also scans the environment to find supporting evidence, based on our thoughts. This is the same part of the brain that creates that phenomenon when we are in the process of buying a new car. We may have just purchased a brand-new vehicle we hadn't noticed on the roads. However, after purchasing the new car, that's all we see on the roads. The RAS is how the law of attraction works—by focusing on what we desire to create that desire.

This part of the brain can easily be fooled by where we place our attention. For example, many people look at our economy and see it as doom and gloom. For many people, that is their reality. However, I am always amazed that statistics showing that every minute a new millionaire appears in our world remain unchanged. That has been true despite the crash in the economy. There is also another reality; new businesses are popping up everywhere I look. My friend, who was laid off, found her new passion in life with a business of her own that she loves. She would not have had the courage to leave her salaried job otherwise.

The point is, from these two realities, we get to choose which one to live in. If you haven't guessed it by now, I will choose the positive one every time. It is our choice to look at life as a crisis or as an opportunity for growth.

The RAS seeks out evidence to support an ingrained thought or belief pattern. For example, let's say we tell ourselves we are stupid and worthless because that is what we were told. If we actively think those thoughts, our brain will naturally seek out and find more and more evidence to support that perception. If you make a mistake and someone calls you out on it, your brain will reinforce your belief that you are stupid and worthless, and this will serve as your "proof." The RAS notices aspects that were always there that we may never have been consciously aware of. As stated earlier, we process approximately four hundred billion bits of information a second. The RAS acts to filter out most of it, except what it perceives as a threat or the things you give focus to. The RAS is similar to a muscle that can be strengthened to help you succeed even more. We allow this cycle to continue running, day in and out. After all, who are we to challenge what we already believe about ourselves and what others have implanted into our minds?

> You are today where your thoughts have brought you;
> you will be tomorrow where your thoughts take you.
> —James Allen

We are the product of our own stories. What are the stories we tell ourselves each day? Think of the ticker on the New York Stock Exchange. The constant flow of information never stops. Our brains have a similar ticker made up of our subconscious self-talk. Thousands and thousands of thoughts sabotage us every second. Most of them are made up from our negative thoughts. Most, if not all, no longer serve us today in our desire to step into our extraordinary being.

I remember growing up with kids who said mean, hurtful,

and hateful words about who they thought I was. *Words have power.* You probably share similar stories; they had it all wrong too. They had no idea who I was, or who you were. Such words debilitate and bring even the strongest kids down through no fault of their own. Everything happens for a reason. Right? These compilations of stories interwoven with words played a vital role in my life. Their words were the motivation I needed to create this die-hard, never-give-up mentality. Yes, they pushed me to excel, to achieve, and to create. What if they hadn't? What I choose today is knowing that this, too, happened for a reason and has brought me here. Amazing, right? I thought you would think that. You are not what people have told you are. If we get to make this choice and choose our new story, what will it be?

I have found that most people are more afraid of success than they are of failure. Failing is easy; success is much more difficult. The people I have worked with have been told over and over what horrible beings they are. Those who have had their self-esteem and confidence stripped away at a young age don't seem to stand a chance (without some significant self-development work).

Too often, we search and search for the evidence to support that somehow we are not good enough. I see this all the time with the amazing people I came in contact with. What I see in them and what they see in themselves are two very different images. In my practice, I have discovered that there really are only a few core issues that people face on a regular basis. These include: I'm not good enough, I'm not worthy, I'm not loved/lovable, I'm not successful, I'm not strong enough, I'm not deserving, and I'm not smart enough.

What is the story you are telling yourself right now?

_____
_____
_____
_____
_____
_____
_____
_____
_____
_____
_____
_____
_____
_____
_____
_____

How is it serving you? (Hint: if that story is in place, it is serving you in some way.)

_____
_____
_____
_____
_____
_____
_____
_____
_____
_____
_____
_____
_____
_____
_____
_____

Is it taking you where you desire to go? □Yes □No

What is driving this story or keeping it in place?

_____

_____

_____

_____

_____

_____

_____

_____

_____

_____

_____

_____

_____

_____

Are you ready to let it go? If not, what are you afraid will happen if you let it go?

_____

_____

_____

_____

_____

_____

_____

_____

_____

_____

_____

_____

Quiet your mind. Take a few deep, cleansing breaths in and out. Ask yourself, "What is it that you are trying to tell me?" Listen to yourself. Did you get an awareness? Did something jump out at you? If so, what was the message? If not, ask again, or try asking, "What prevents me from having an awareness of this?"

Journal here.

_____

_____

_____

_____

_____

_____

_____

_____

_____

_____

_____

_____

_____

_____

Words have power. Words make up our world. We speak them, we hear them, we sing them, we write them, we react and respond to them, we process our environment and our experiences through them. Everything is given meaning through them.

Words have power. Our thoughts are powerful. After all, they are words, and the more focus we give them, the more powerful they become. We are powerful and potent beings when creating. When we free up the negative energy from our past, we allow ourselves to be free to create.

I look around and I see examples of negativity everywhere. I'm sitting at lunch when I overhear a father and brother tease the girl sitting with them about her looks. I'm listening. I know that their intentions were meant to be playful. But when she quickly quieted and drew inward, I know those words had sunk to a deeper level. She is not alone. We all do this from time to time.

Words have power. What we tell ourselves matters. While visiting the United States, the Dalai Lama stated how sad it was to see that people in the United States carried so much hate toward themselves and others. He was actually unaware of the term *self-hate* until someone described it to him. Have we become conditioned to think the worst of ourselves and others? When we live with a negative worldview, make judgments, and jump to conclusions, it shuts off our energy flow, just like that. By shifting this paradigm, we create a powerful place for self-love to flourish, no longer controlled by fear, anxiety, and hate.

In my practice, self-talk is one of the major areas I work with people on. So many of the individuals I work with are just like you and I. Almost everyone has been affected by and are often living their lives based on the stories picked up along their journey. We have all received, whether we like it or not, messages from those around us. These messages may have been overtly or covertly delivered and received consciously or subconsciously by us. These messages have extreme power over us. We will even find ourselves changing our lives based on these messages without realizing it. We continue to sabotage our own lives to give life to the stories that keep us small.

I'll give you an example. In elementary school I was never fond of standing up and giving oral book reports. I was not a fan of public speaking, which I quickly learned I was not even remotely skilled at. I received message after message, mostly from my teachers, that reinforced the notion that I was a terrible public speaker. This message continued through high school and then into college. One professor stated, "You are so nervous that you make me nervous just listening to you." That message may have been intended to be constructive criticism, but all I heard was, "You suck!" I internally translated that into "I am a terrible public speaker." That was my evidence. This belief was so strongly planted in my being that it was nearly impossible to remove it. As you can imagine, I did not grow up and go into public speaking. Why? The messages I received starting when I was a small child were vividly planted in my mind and supported by overwhelming evidence. When I learned the concepts in this book, I started to undo the damage. I confronted previous fears and stories that were not mine in the first place. As I started to work on my own head trash and limiting beliefs around public speaking, I realized I had a profound passion for public speaking. Imagine that! Me, a public speaker. I had to work on myself to unlock the root of the messages I had been feeding myself for years and re-create my story. If I could do this, you can too.

Exercise
Take a minute and think about your recent thoughts. Where are they focused? Are they focused on something you have done that's phenomenal, or do they drift toward areas where you "should have" or "could have" done

better? You might be surprised to see how negative your thoughts really are. It's easy to beat ourselves up: "That was so stupid of me"; "What was I thinking?", or "Why did I just do that?" When we get lost in these thoughts, the body creates a negative physiological response that includes increased heart rate, elevated blood pressure, tightened muscles, and dilated pupils. When our bodies and our minds get in this place it is difficult to get out of the muck. But what if something else is possible?

Barbara Fredrickson is a positive psychology researcher from the University of North Carolina who has provided insights into how negative thinking impacts the brain. According to her research, negative emotions narrow your mind and focus your thoughts. As a result, you are unable to see all the options and possibilities in a situation. When we were faced with daily threats, such as wild animals, in prehistoric times, this was an important function. However, in modern society the need to protect ourselves from the threat of meeting a tiger on the daily walk to the store is no longer relevant. But the brain is still programmed to respond in this manner, limiting our ability to see possibilities. On the other hand, Fredrickson also discovered the "broaden and build" theory that states that positive emotions broaden your sense of possibilities, which in turn allows you to build new tools and skills.

It is always our choice what we choose to think about. What are we placing our attention? Napoleon Hill said, "Positive and negative emotions cannot occupy the mind at the same time. One or the other must dominate. It is your responsibility to make sure that positive emotions constitute the dominating influence of your mind." The power of this lies within the choices we make. Words have power, and so do our thoughts, because they determine how the law of attraction will work. But when our thoughts become distorted, it leads to challenges in the way in which we experience our world, reinforcing what we place our focus on. Here is a list of limiting thought distortions to watch out for.

Automatic Thought Distortions
All or nothing thinking: seeing everything in black or white, with no ability to see the whole picture, viewing the world with an either/or mentality. "If I'm not perfect, then I am a failure."

Assuming: we assume the worst case scenario without testing out the evidence first. "You are angry at me." Or "I did something wrong."

Blaming: the opposite of personalizing. We blame other people or situations instead of taking personal responsibility for our part. "She has ruined my life.

Catastrophizing: the "snowball" experience, when you expect the worst to happen and then blow it out of proportion. "It's going to be disaster, and they are going to hate me for it."

Dwelling on the negative: involves focusing on the negative evidence, refusing to see the positive in any situation. "My wedding is ruined because it snowed."

Jumping to conclusions: without checking out all of the facts of the situation, you automatically determine how others are going to feel or respond to you. "She is going to hate this idea."

Labeling or mislabeling: the extreme form of

overgeneralizing. Attaching a negative label to yourself, someone else, or something you have done. "I'm stupid." Or "He is so lazy."

Making feelings facts: Making your feelings the evidence for how everything is. "I feel inadequate. I must be inadequate."

Overgeneralizing: taking a negative experience and generalizing it to other experiences or outcomes. Using words like *always*, *never*, *no one*, etc. "I will never be good enough."

Personalizing: seeing yourself as the root cause for a negative external event or situation that happened. "It's all my fault."

Rejecting the positive: dismissing or negating the positive aspects of a situation, as if they do not count. "This old thing? It's been in my closet for years." This is common in accepting personal compliments.

Shoulds, Musts, Oughts): the demands that we make on ourselves that ultimately leave us feeling frustrated at the situation. "I should have known better." Or "She should have apologized."

The fairy-tale fantasy: demanding high expectations from life. This is a special type of *should*. "The world shouldn't be this way."

Unfavorable comparisons: when you amplify your faults and minimize your strengths. "I still work for a company, but she is a successful entrepreneur"

Many people are faced with the challenge of trying to

manage the inner workings of their minds. Let's face it. It can sometimes be enough to just get through the day, let alone understanding the make-up of our thoughts and the impact that they have upon our lives. I get it! Still, it is of critical importance that we begin to pay attention to how we think and why we think that way. Many of us get stuck in the rumination trap. You know the one; you keep processing the same thought over and over again from five thousand different angles, only to keep arriving at the same destination, only to find yourself deeper in the muck and feeling even more hopeless and powerless.

What is the value in these negative thoughts?

Become cognizant of your negative thoughts and the messages they give you, the feelings they generate. What else do they trigger for you? Thoughts provoke various emotions in our bodies. Our feelings are an internal guidance system that is designed to provide us with information to understand our world.

Our thoughts are powerful, but we have the power to change them at any given moment. This takes practice, but it can be done. Our default modes can be shifted to thoughts that allow our authentic selves to shine. Letting go of our self-doubt, self-sabotage, and self-deprecation is the beginning of the path toward our truth.

Freeing ourselves from the muck means moving beyond self-hate to a place of self-love. A place where we can accept ourselves, without judgment, criticism, and doubt. I realize that after being in the muck for so long, ingrained with these negative views of ourselves, letting go of this negative self-identity may be scary and disorienting. Just know and have faith that you will be rebuilt, stronger and better than ever! It's time. It's time for you to step into your extraordinary self! Yes!

Digging out of the muck. Learning to love yourself again. Words have power. Let's start there, with the words we tell ourselves that create the world we live in.

Create a list of the qualities that you bring to this world that you *like* about yourself.

Sit with this for a day or two and review often.

Now, create a list of the qualities that you bring to this world that you *love* about yourself.

☐ _____

☐ _____

☐ _____

☐ _____

☐ _____

☐ _____

☐ _____

☐ _____

☐ _____

☐ _____

II is time to let other people's perspectives of us be just that—their opinions, not ours. We are all different, and that is a *wonderful* thing! I am so grateful that you have been brought to this world as a unique individual, because your gifts are different than mine, your neighbors, your families, and everyone else's. That is what makes you special. We all deserve to be special. This is part of self-acceptance. Embrace your beautiful quirks. Thoughts do not have power over us until we give them that power. If we are going to have the same thoughts every day, why not make them *work* for us?

According to Sonja Lyubomirsky, positive words and thoughts have a direct impact on the motivational center of the brain that launches it into action and supports building resilience when we are face life's problems. Her research has identified the multitude of benefits from happiness. Abraham Lincoln stated, "Most folks are as happy as they want to be." Meaning that each of us have a choice in our own happiness. We can always choose the state in which we live in.

"I'm not good enough." "What will people think of me? "No one will like/love me." "What if I fail?" "Why me?" "I'm stupid; I'm a complete failure." "No one understands me." "I'm such a joke." "I can't." "I should know this." "Why does it have to be so hard?" "I'm never going to get this. "I'm such a failure." Plus all the millions of other versions that are not serving you now. It's time to shift. It's time for you to start showing up in this world.

Creating new stories consists of discovering ourselves from within. The late Dr. Wayne Dyer spoke of how changing the way we feel allows us to change our reality. Create your new story, and feel those feelings of having already created it as often as you can. When the programmed tape inside your brain starts to play the story of worry, doubt, uncertainty, fear, and judgment, choose a new story. I know that, personally speaking, when I run the tape of my new story, I cannot help but shift myself to a new place of hope, possibility, and, most of all, joy.

It's time to get out of the way. The power is in embracing the positive side of life. This is what I call living deliciously! This is the fun part, when you are in the flow, when you feel happy and filled with energy, when everything is falling into place beautifully. You are in touch with your inner genius; you walk with an extra bounce in you step and feel like you can create and generate *anything*!

In the beginning, my thoughts trapped me and kept me from seeing my true potential. By challenging this paradigm in which we live, we can be anything, do anything, and have anything we desire.

You get to choose the stories you tell yourself.

Examples new stories

- I am abundant.
- I am a powerful woman, and I know that anything is possible.
- I am love.
- I empower those around me to succeed.
- I am passionate about life.
- I easily and effortlessly take on challenges because I know this makes me grow wiser.
- I am the creator of my own reality.
- I choose my life.
- I allow my silly quirks and playfulness to be seen.
- I choose happiness.
- I play hard.
- I find laughter in each day.
- I spend my time with those I love and care about.
- I am a giver and an excellent receiver.
- I ask for support when I desire it.
- I create a positive impact on other people's lives.
- I inspire and empower them to discover their greatness within.
- I take advantage of all life has to offer.
- I fill myself with the energy of the universe.
- I allow myself to be patient with this amazing process.
- I am curious about life.
- I seek our exciting adventures.
- I am abundant.

What is the new story that *you* get to create?

_____

_____

_____

_____

_____

_____

_____

_____

_____

_____

_____

_____

_____

_____

_____

_____

It feels amazing to create. Right? Can I get some heel-clicks please? Wahoo!

Avoiding the Trap

When we start eliminating head trash one belief at a time, we ultimately start shifting our perspectives out of the muck. We start seeing the possibilities, the gifts, and the lessons we were meant to learn. We start finding ways to extend our time in this positive state of being that aligns more authentically with our true selves. This is the place that people call the "easy life," or what I call our "zone of brilliance." It is the magical state of being that allows you to create and generate with total ease. Everything seems to fall into place beautifully, people show up in your life with serendipity, and you feel fully alive!

LIVING EXTRAORDINARY

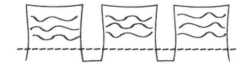

With almost everyone I have worked with, there is a time period when they vacillate between these two worlds until they have worked through the beliefs that once held them back. This is the place of transition where transformation begins.

TRANSITION

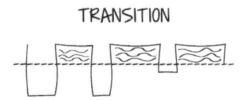

I used to think that living above the line was the target to create in my life. Although that is important, what I discovered in my own work with people the most crucial element of the entire transition was the space between these two states at each intersectional point. What I mean by this is learning to recognize what is taking place when we are free from the muck and when we are being sucked back into it. (See the Intersectional points diagram.) The magic can be found by understanding how you "lose it" and how you "gain it" back. Once this has been mastered, the power you bring to this world can finally be unleashed in an intentional and powerful way. I can't tell you how many people have walked out of my office saying, "I can't explain it, but I feel magical!"

I simply smile, knowing they have just tapped into their magic within.

INTERSECTIONAL POINTS

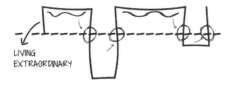

LIVING
EXTRAORDINARY

I was speaking to a mentor years and years ago. I told him how much I loved living in the high-on-life state of being and asked why couldn't I live there all the time. He said, "No one can keep up that state forever." He explained that monks who meditate for days on end eventually will lose that state, but the key is to know how to return to it. Over the years my week of transition turned into three days, which turned into one day. Now it's five minutes tops. Learning to master the space in between is truly where all the work is and is the key to total transformation.

However, I must warn you as you start this transition process of leaving the muck behind for good, your subconscious and unconscious minds are *not* going to be happy. I am not kidding you. Let's think about this. Your subconscious and unconscious minds have been in charge for decades, and your attempt to change this is going to be met with great resistance. You might even want to give up. Don't! Something greater is waiting for you on the other side. I promise you. I will ask you to use the tools in this book twice as often each day, because the fight will become your greatest challenge. When you start to change the trajectory of your life, you will sometimes find yourself feeling worse than you did before you took this leap of faith outside your comfort zone.

You may find yourself in unexplained circumstances that feel much worse. You get a flat tire, have a car accident, lose your favorite pair of shoes, get a parking ticket, bounce a check, get into fight with your best friend, etc. In reality, this chaos is created to sabotage you and keep everything at status quo. This is the moment you are asked, "How badly do you want it?" The universe is going to question you. Are you all in or just dipping your toe in? Any person who has gone through this knows that it often gets worse before we are fully able to stand in our brilliance and shine. We have spent our lives creating the reality that we live in, so why wouldn't we be faced with a strong pull to stay that way? When we choose to live our extraordinary lives and pull ourselves out of the depths of the muck, we place ourselves on the path of rewiring the nueropathways in our brain. This takes time and perseverance. It's not an easy process at first, but it does get easier. Taking risks and trusting that everything happens for a reason will grow you more than you can imagine. No matter what happens, just remember where you are coming from and where you are heading. *You can* do this! Keep pushing through!

One of my greatest joys is gently showing the women and men I have worked with in my practice the way to pull themselves out of the muck so they can breathe again. One of the amazing women I worked with came from an unthinkable past that had her shackled and chained. She came in every week trying to convince me that she was a terrible, awful, unlovable person. I didn't buy it for a second, and I challenged her every day about this. I'm pretty sure there were days she wanted to kick me, but I wasn't backing down to play the game she had so masterfully been engaging in for all her adult years. Just when I started to think we were not making the progress I so eagerly wanted for her, there it was. The shift. It came as such a surprise to her that she actually didn't even recognize it. It started with one sentence that was filled with hope, wrapping her soul with joy for the first time. There it was. As I pointed out this shift in perspective, which was delivered in a positive framework, she began to see the first glimpse into her profoundly changed new life. We continued our work as she vacillated between her old truth and her new truth, like a game of tug-o-war. At one point she began to own her new truth and embrace it like never before. She was finally free to go explore her life with a new set of lenses. I told her, "You are free to fire me. My job is done." As I write this, her story, like so many others I have encountered over the years, has truly been my why.

What to do when you are wallowing in the muck?

Stop. Stop what you are doing. The power of the law attraction is not on your side when you are going in a negative direction. Stop what you are doing and leave where you are. Change your atmosphere to help change your thinking. A good friend came to the rescue for me once. In a panicked state, I called her to explain how *everything* was falling apart. After some great support, I had to ask one more favor. "Do you mind staying on the phone with me while I close down the office?" Although she had already talked me off the cliff, I knew that if I hung up I wouldn't hold myself to leaving the office. When I hung up, the workaholic in me would have gone back to trying to fix what I was so easily destroying. With that final touch of support, I stopped *everything* and left. I went home early, ran a few miles, and I relaxed, knowing that tomorrow I would start fresh and new again. We are powerful and potent beings in either direction.

- Get support. I know that you are probably a go-getter and that you can go it alone, but you don't need or have to. I'm giving everyone permission right now to seek out support. I recommend venting for a few minutes when you feel the urge, and then start looking for the gifts in that experience to help shift your thinking.
- Journal. Keep a journal of all your limiting thoughts each day (you may be surprised at how often you are in this place). Replace with a more reasonable response (if you were giving your best friend advice on this, what would you say?). Create a plan and work on eliminating those self-disparaging thoughts for good. Check out all the tools in this book!
- Exercise. We all know the health benefits of exercise for our physique, but what we have perhaps underestimated is the numerous ways in which it benefits the brain. According to experts, physical exercise releases feel-good chemicals, improving memory and increasing mental focus. A fun experiment involves setting a goal or asking yourself a question, then letting go and exercising. Whenever I do this, I always come away with an answer or solution and increased clarity. Try it, and let me know how it works out for you.
- Movement. This is one of the quickest ways to shift your state of mind. Try this. Stand up and shake out your body. Yes, shake out your legs, arms, and torso. If you are like most people, you are probably silly, and chances are really good that you just made yourself smile, if not laugh. You just shifted your energy!

- Let go. This takes practice. Through the act of letting go and releasing yourself from outcomes, solutions, situation, etc., you begin to free yourself. When I let go of things, I use a physical reminder to make it more concrete. I quickly and forcibly rub both of my hands together in a wiping motion to signify that I'm done and I am letting this go. This comes in handy in circumstances I have no control over.

We are infinite beings. *Everything* that we need to succeed is already within us

I give you permission to start eliminating your head trash. Become aware of the self-limiting thoughts and stories that keep you playing small and stuck in the muck. I give you permission to step into your full potential, be extraordinary, and come to discover your purpose, power, and prosperous being, to create, discover, and share your passion with the world. Others will celebrate your arrival. Be grateful, and look for a rainbow at the end of your storm. Remember. Life is what you make of it. Head trash left unemptied impairs vision and sets limits upon your destiny built by fear and failure. Aim to rid your mind of head trash, because in the end, you hold the keys to unlocking personal success

> " We are infinite beings. *Everything* that we need to succeed is already within us. "

The quest to eliminate head trash is a personal journey that you must master by determining what works best for you. Here are some strategies to help you along the way:

Eliminating Your Head Trash Toolbox

Interesting Point of View Exercise: We tend to feed our brain with such negativity that we find it hard to dig ourselves out from under it all. What happens is that negativity is reinforced in the brain, as we learned earlier in this chapter. Here is a great tool to help cancel out the negativity and create more positive conscious thought that serves us better today. Repeat: "Interesting point of view that I have this interesting point of view" (Access Consciousness). Say this three times for every negative thought, judgment, or conclusion you have come to. This is a powerful tool. I have people start doing it immediately to avoid taking on any further negative thoughts that ultimately turn into beliefs. Considering how many unconscious thoughts we have in a day, the more you do this the better. Try ten thousand times a day. I'm exaggerating a little bit, but I want you to get the point.

Follow this exercise with a question to open the energy back up. "What else is possible?"

EFT Script: Getting yourself out of the way/Eliminating head trash
https://vimeo.com/talkingwithteri/outoftheway

For best results, tune into a particular negative thought or story that has been blocking you and your success as you go through the sequences provided.

To start: Rate yourself on a scale from zero to ten: ten equals worst; zero equals best. Where would you rate yourself on your head trash or negative thinking?

Tap on the karate chop point while saying the following:

- Even though this negativity runs my life, I deeply and completely love and accept myself.
- Even though my brain has learned this way of thinking and I have believed these stories for years, I deeply and completely love and accept myself.
- Even though this negativity is a part of me, I deeply and completely love and accept myself.

Round 1 (Negative Reminder phrases):

H: All of this negativity and doubt that consumes my life,
EB: All of this negativity that drains my soul and keeps me from my authentic self,
SE: I couldn't possibly let it go. Who would I be?
UE: I choose to know that I am in safe in letting it go.
UN: What if I could let it go?

Key:

H=Head
EB=Eyebrow
SE=Side of eye
UE=Under eye
UN=Under nose
CH=Chin
CB=Collarbone
UA=Under arm

CH: I choose to know that I can be open, open to allowing so much more into my life.

CB: I allow myself to be open, open to all the billions of possibilities

UA: Yes! I allow myself to be open to all the positives I am creating.

Round 2 (Positive phrases):
**Repeat as needed

H: I am open to seeing the positives in my life.

EB: I choose to embrace all of me as the person I know I am.

SE: I am positive. I am my own creator of my reality.

UE: I allow positivity into my life with ease and joy.

UN: I trust in myself that everything will be taken care of.

CH: Peace fills my body, spirit, soul.

CB: I am in allowance of my greatness ... starting now.

UA: I allow myself to see the gifts in my life easily and effortlessly.

Continue going through this sequence until you reach zero.

Chapter 4

Expand Outside Your Comfort Zone

Unless you try to do something beyond what you
have already mastered, you will never grow.
—Ralph Waldo Emerson

Take risks. Go on, you daredevil, you!

Nothing extraordinary was ever achieved by playing it
safe. Greatness comes with taking the next steps without
having it all perfectly figured out. Have you allowed
yourself to become comfortable or complacent? Take a
look around your life. Have you settled for a mediocre job
so you don't have to step outside of what you now know?
Have you learned to be comfortable with extra weight
gain by making justifications for it? Have you learned
to be comfortable with worrying about everyone else's
happiness except yours? Have you settled for believing
that everyone else deserves joy, love, success, but not
you? Have you learned that it is okay to lose your voice,
your passion, and your purpose because "I'm not good
enough" to have it? Settling can often be the truth on the
dark side of the thing we call the comfort zone.

We are creatures of habit. Have you ever attended a two- or
three-day workshop where there was no assigned seating?

The first day you go in and select your seat. The following day, same seat, and on the third day, the same. Why? It's comfortable. We don't have to go out of our way to find a new place to sit, meet more unfamiliar people, make small talk before getting settled. It's just easy to keep sitting where we have already been. However, try this on at the next workshop. Arrive early the second day and change out your seat. You will find other people have a difficult time with the situation and feel uncomfortable or, worse, seem put off by change in course. We are creatures of habit.

When we stay in that pattern of sameness, our brain fires the same exact same way, all the time, every day. When we choose something different, we actually change the neuropathways of the brain. Neuroplasticity is the ability of the brain to adapt to new information we have learned. Changing pathways requires us to enter a state of the unknown, which isn't always easy, given our creature-of-habit tendencies.

Where are you finding yourself remaining comfortable for fear of trying something new? (Health, career, relationships, family, education, etc.).

_____

_____

_____

_____

_____

_____

_____

_____

_____

_____

_____

_____

_____

_____

_____

Growth cannot take place until we move beyond what we have always known. Any improvement in our lives requires a leap of faith into the unknown that lies outside your comfort zone. This is the time to shift anxiety and fear into excitement over exploration. It is all perspective, right?

I never knew what was on other side of my comfort zone until I took a leap of faith to find out. The more steps I've taken to get out of my comfort zone, the wider the circumference has spread.

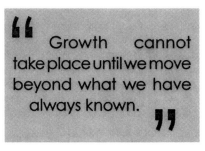

> Growth cannot take place until we move beyond what we have always known.

Stepping out of the comfort zone requires understanding that we are constantly growing, changing, and shifting out of old mindsets. It takes courage to step into a new way of living that requires us to learn more tools and skills along the way. It is safe and it is easy to stay within that which you already know. It takes courage to go where you have never been before. In business and in life, I have observed that those who travel outside their limitations grow beyond their imaginations. Doing things differently is imperative to seeing different results. The space just outside of our comfort zone is truly our zone of brilliance. This is where the magic happens. This is where possibilities are transformed into a reality.

It starts with putting your risks into perspective. Often when I ask people what holds them back from doing

XYZ, they say, "Fear of XYZ." But if fear is learned; it can be unlearned.

Marianne Williamson says, "Love is what we are born with. Fear is what we learn." Think back to risks you have taken in the past. Do you still feel that the world was going to end by taking that leap of faith? If you are anything like me, the answer is, "Probably not." I recall the day I went into private practice, thinking that I was making the biggest choice of my life; now I look back and think, Wow. That was nothing compared to the risks that I am taking now.

The number one reason for staying inside your comfort zone is fear. Fear of the unknown. What if the unknown is something incredible to be discovered? What if the unknown is a billion possibilities waiting at your fingertips? Someone once asked me, "If we had all the answers and our lives were always as planned, would life be worth living?" If we knew it all, wouldn't that take out all the mystery and fun? Food for thought.

You may be telling yourself at this very moment, "I have no desire to leave my comfort zone." Or maybe, "I'm perfectly content where I am." And that might very well be the case. I am hoping to reach those of you who question whether or not there is more to life than the one you are currently living and those of you who are not living the ten that you deserve to be living. If you are in love with your life and you are fully living the life of your dreams, you get it. I hope that this serves as a reminder to you to keep moving in the direction of your life's passion and purpose.

According to the *Harvard Mental Health Letter* of

December 2004, newborns are born with only two natural fears. Yes, I said two! Fear of falling and fear of loud noises. *Everything else* is learned! I find this extremely fascinating. As I look around, I see fear *everywhere*. The absolutely amazing piece of information is that fear is *learned*. Therefore, it can be *unlearned*.

Here's an established acronym for fear:

> F: false
> E: expectations
> A: appearing
> R: real

Fear is nothing new. Harvard physiologist Walter Cannon discovered the flight-or-fight response in the early 1900s. Fear is simply a reaction to a stressful stimulus that releases chemicals in our bodies that increase heart rate, blood pressure, breathing, and muscle tension, to name a few. This response is almost entirely an unconscious automatic response. The stimulus may include a number of situations, events, or experiences, from hearing a loud noise to seeing a snake. Due to our cultural norms, now most people find themselves living in a state of constant stress. Our bodies assume that we are under attack and respond as such. This signals the brain that we are always "on." In the wild, our bodies are designed to go from a state of fear to a state of calm once the stressor has been removed. This allows our bodies to repair. Not returning to this more peaceful state has been linked to a host of medical conditions. Some researchers state that approximately 90 percent of all chronic illness, aliments, and diseases can be traced back to the root cause of stress and its effects on the body.

When we allow ourselves to live in fear, we activate stress hormones in the body. When we focus long enough on troubled memories, doom and gloom about the future, or things that we cannot control, we inevitably prevent our bodies from returning to a state of homeostasis.

The emotional response to fear allows our body to respond to a perceived threat. We are born with this built-in mechanism. Thousands of years ago, when we were faced with threats from dangerous animals that ruled the land or other dangerous situations, there was a clear purpose for this emotional response. It kept us safe. But we have taken this innate response to a whole new level in modern times, allowing our thoughts to launch our bodies into this flight-or-fight response unnecessarily. In her book *Positively Fearless*, Vera Peiffer explores how contemporary fear appears to be in relation to what we think might happen to us versus experiences that are actually happening.

To understand how fear holds us back, look no further than our internal thoughts. What if I don't get this job promotion? What if I bomb this talk? "What if no one calls me back? These thoughts set the stage for increasing fear and stress. Based on the law of attraction, we are subconsciously creating more stressful experiences. This is how many people get stuck in the muck in the first place.

Fear is teachable. I think that we have been unintentionally teaching fear for decades.

Some researchers say that we start to live in fear in the first five years of life. On a visit to a park a couple years ago, my daughter and I marveled at the ants as they picked at a half-eaten cracker on the ground. I am always in awe of ants. I'm pretty sure I could spend the entire day watching them and never tire of it. On this particular day, a random mother and her twin three-year-old girls joined us at the picnic bench. Their experience was different than ours. When the girls ran screaming toward the ants, at first I thought it was excitement, but as they began stomping and killing the ants I knew that could not to be true. My daughter ran to me and asked, "Why are they smashing the ants?" The mom looked at me with a horrified look. "I just hate bugs of any sort." Now, who did that fear belong to? What fears are we teaching our children, family, friends, colleagues, etc., every day?

Fear is what holds people back from allowing themselves to achieve their goals. If you don't believe me, test it yourself. Ask people what their ultimate dreams are and if they know without a doubt that they can achieve them. Then ask what keeps them from having achieved their dreams by now. Sit back and just wait for the "but" disguised as an excuse. I have found that this question is typically answered with either a fear that keeps it from happening or an excuse to avoid taking action.

If we live in fear, then we are living in either the past or in the future, not the present moment. Fear has served a purpose in our lives. Holding onto it doesn't. We create the reality in which we live. What if we conditioned ourselves so that *fear* stands for:

> F: feeling
> E: ecstatic
> A: and
> R: rocking it!

It's not as farfetched as you might think. Fear can also be

excitement. The fascinating aspect of our bodies is that from a physiological perspective, fear manifests in our bodies in the same way as excitement does. Knowing this, we can reframe our experience to harness this energy for a positive impact in our lives.

Fear Versus Excitement

Anxiety/Fear	Excitement
• Racing thoughts	• Racing thoughts
• Increased heart rate	• Increased heart rate
• Increased body energy	• Increased body energy
• Increased adrenaline	• Increased adrenaline
• Muscles feel weak	• Muscles feel weak
• Difficult to concentrate	• Difficult to concentrate
• Not able to eat	• Not able to eat
• Increased breathing rate	• Increased breathing rate

It is all perspective. We are in charge of giving either perspective power. If you get to choose, which will you choose? Keep in mind that the RAS will find the evidence to support either these choices.

How much of what we have been calling fear is actually excitement in disguise? I remember taking a huge leap when I signed a lease that tripled my current space. In many ways, it freaked me out. Thoughts like, What am I doing? How am I going to make this work? and the like began pumping through my head. I had to take a step back and look at it from a different perspective. "Wow, this is exciting! Look what we are creating! We are growing, expanding!" If my body is going to experience the same response to fear as it does to excitement, I choose the latter. Let's tie in the law of attraction and our emotions in relation to the law of attraction. More excitement attracts more excitement; more fear attracts more fear.

Taking risks undoubtedly requires courage. It also requires an mind open to unlimited possibilities. Taking risks allows us to step into our true gifts in this world. While some of the risks I have taken have been carefully planned out, others have been—well, let's say a little more haphazard. The common denominator, though, is this: I rely a lot on faith— faith in myself and faith in my ability to make choices, no matter the risk. This faith has grown stronger with each roll of the dice and has undergone an evolution all its own as it gradually shifted to sure-footed knowledge—the knowledge that things will always work out. When we start taking steps out of our comfort zone, we begin to tolerate more and more discomfort, and soon we are miles from where we began.

Outside The Comfort Zone

Some people may not feel ready or prepared to take risks. Making choices without having all the answers beforehand is a characteristic that drives some people to give up before they ever see their efforts come to fruition. Fear is often the culprit that paralyzes us so we remain within the confines of our comfort zone. When I am working with clients, not playing full-out is their biggest regret in life. What is the opposite of living extraordinary? Living in mediocrity. Mediocrity is the new norm, quite literally.

I think a note of caution is warranted here. I'm not saying to go out and take crazy, irresponsible, and careless risks just for the sake of it. Running off to Vegas and blowing your life savings is not the brightest of ideas. I am talking about taking smaller and even free risks to move beyond the status quo.

I give you permission to allow your knowingness to guide you, even if you have not figured it all out. It is important to recognize that taking a chance and stepping outside of your comfort zone may not always mean you experience immediate success. We sometimes fail in order to learn how to get back up and do it a little bit differently the next time. As Thomas Edison once said, "I have not failed. I have merely found ten thousand ways that won't work."

Thomas Edison and others like him who took tremendous risks inspire me daily. Napoleon Hill, Rosa Parks, Amelia Earhart, and Abraham Lincoln, to name just a few, have made tremendous impact on the world around them. One common quality I have discovered from studying influential and successful individuals is that that they all took fierce risks, not always knowing how it was going to pan out. *You* can do it too!

Reflection
Take a minute to think about your greatest achievement or pivotal moment in your life. What type of risk did it involve?

_____

_____

_____

_____

_____

_____

_____

_____

_____

_____

_____

_____

_____

_____

_____

Taking risks outside our comfort zone requires us to grow beyond what we thought was possible.

Personal Growth May Lie Ahead exercise

Take a minute to complete this quick exercise. Clasp your hands together in front of you. Notice which thumb is on top. Now interlace your fingers and allow the other thumb to be on top. Feels weird, right?

In this exercise, several things happened. You left your comfort zone and did something different that fired new neurons in your brain. Even though it felt different or weird, you tried something new that gave you evidence that change was safe. Showing courage means not knowing how it is all going to work out and being vulnerable anyway.

Here are a few ideas to get you started in taking yourself outside your comfort zone.

Getting Out of Your Comfort Zone exercises

Try taking a new way home. What did you notice?

_____

_____

_____

_____

_____

_____

_____

_____

_____

_____

_____

_____

_____

Identify a small, fun adventure you have always desired to try. Take some inspired action to schedule and complete it. What did you learn?

_____

_____

_____

_____

_____

_____

_____

_____

_____

_____

_____

_____

It's your turn. Fill in the blank._____
What did you notice?

When we step into the unknown we risk a level of vulnerability. Brene Brown is a research professor at the University of Houston Graduate College of Social Work; she has become a leading expert on vulnerability. Her work has transformed the way we look at vulnerability. According to her research, *vulnerability* is defined as uncertainty, risk, and emotional exposure. She adds that vulnerability is not knowing victory or defeat, it is understanding the necessity of both; it's engaging. It's being all in. I listened to Dr. Brown during a speaking engagement, and she stated that vulnerability means allowing ourselves to open up our hearts and take risks. After all, it takes courage to step outside of our comfort zone, be vulnerable, and begin your path of massive expansion.

In the movie *We Bought a Zoo*, what stuck with me was when the main character said, "I just need twenty seconds of courage." What if we allowed ourselves this brief moment—twenty seconds—for what could turn out to be profound and defining moments in our lives? Taking risks undoubtedly requires courage; it also requires a mind open to unlimited possibilities. Mark Twain said, "Courage is the mastery of fear, not the absence of fear."

We can greatly reduce fear when we hold on to our faith in ourselves. Did you ever have a feeling that everything was just going to work out? You didn't know how, but you just knew, deep down in your soul?

Hold on to Faith

Holding onto faith requires us to step into a knowingness that is larger than ourselves. No matter what your beliefs, the true test in life is allowing ourselves to simply trust the process. I'm speaking from a previous control-freak mindset. Letting go of the need to control has been a life-long learning process. The greatest lessons in my life have followed moments in which I was required to hold on to an unwavering faith in the universe and allow transformation to take place, to be completely vulnerable and allow the pieces of my life to fall together beautifully. It meant giving up control, the need to figure it all out, and to have all the answers. It is without a doubt the greatest gift to one's self.

Faith allows us to foster a belief that anything is possible. In doing so, you allow yourself to go beyond self-imposed limitations and step outside your comfort zone. When you begin to have faith in yourself and your own abilities, you will find yourself doing things that used to intimidate you, and you will begin to stretch and grow. In fact, you become a person who creates and exudes confidence and success.

I give you permission to not have it all figured out and to instead allow your knowingness to guide you. It is important to recognize that in taking a chance and stepping outside of our comfort zone we may not always experience immediate success. However, the lessons that we learn allow us to level up in life and we are greater beings for it. As Thomas Edison once said, "I have not failed. I have merely found 10,000 ways that won't work." So I give you permission to expand beyond what your thought was possible.

Get Out of My Comfort Zone Toolbox
We all have a range of behaviors, feelings, and attitudes that we feel comfortable with. It's human nature to stay within this zone and rarely step into unknown territory. So the first thing I advise people to do is to take one small step outside it every day. For example, if you dread or usually avoid making a cold call, make just one today. The more you grow and expand your comfort zone, the easier it is to take bigger steps outside of the comfort zone.

- Practice spontaneity. Life doesn't always need to be planned out.
- Educate yourself about whatever it is you fear. You will be surprised that some of those things are not as scary as they seem. I was once told to think of a worst-case scenario; "If you can live with that, then go for it! Chances are that you will be far from that worst-case point.

- Create a tenacious can-do attitude. Start surrounding yourself with people who share a similar outlook and believe that *anything* is possible!
- Get in the practice of shaking up your routine (i.e., drive home a new way). This step begins to create new neuropathways in the brain, which also increases your overall confidence that anything is possible!
- Create a Victory Log. Write down all your successes related to getting out of your comfort zone and then reference it when doubt, fear, or uncertainty sets in. It's the proof you can do it again!
- Write out one hundred adventures. Make a list of one hundred things you would like to try or do in your lifetime. I recommend limiting the places where you want to travel to the top ten. There might easily be one hundred places you could write down. Each month or week do one of the things on your list. This gives you something exciting to look forward to, but it also starts moving you outside of your comfort zone in a fun way.
- Create your Bucket List. Create a list of one hundred things you desire to do in your life. It can span all areas of your life: romantic, professional, and/or spiritual. This gives you an opportunity to really ask yourself what your goals are. You might be surprised by what you reveal to yourself.
- Try something new every day. Even if it's small; maybe try a new food for the first time. The best way to break the habit of ordinary is to *do something different.*
- Ask yourself: "What if this turns out better than I ever planned or imagined?"
- EFT script. See below

EFT Script: Get outside the comfort zone, release the fear
https://vimeo.com/talkingwithteri/comfortzone

To start: Rate yourself on a scale from zero to ten. Ten equals worst; zero equals best. Where would you rate yourself on getting outside your comfort zone?

Tap on the karate chop point while saying the following:

- Even though I'm terrified to get outside of my comfort zone, I deeply and completely love and accept myself.
- Even though I have held myself back for so long I don't know what my next step is, I deeply and completely love and accept myself.
- Even though it's scary and exciting all at the same time, I deeply and completely love and accept myself.

Round 1 (Negative Reminder phrases):

H: I am terrified to step outside my comfort zone.

EB: What if something bad happens? What if something amazing happens?

SE: I just can't. Yes, I can. No, I can't. *Yes!* Yes, I *can!*

UE: I forgive myself for any time I have not taken risks based on my fears.

UN: I forgive anyone else for anything that they have done to keep me from taking these risks based on their fears.

Key:

H=Head
EB=Eyebrow
SE=Side of eye
UE=Under eye
UN=Under nose
CH=Chin
CB=Collarbone
UA=Under arm

CH: I give myself permission to live out loud and embrace all of me!

CB: I am safe in expanding my comfort zone again and again.

UA: I am an ever-expanding being.

Round 2 (Positive phrases):
**Repeat as needed

H: I am open to all the possibilities in my life.

EB: I allow and step into what it would be like to live with courage.

SE: I am safe in creating my amazing life.

UE: I choose to know that I can be safe when stepping out into the unknown.

UN: I am safe. I allow my life to be filled with ease, joy, and glory.

CH: I forgive myself for shrinking to fit in all these years.

CB: I am free to expand and be expansive.

UA: I forgive myself for shrinking to fit in all these years. I am an expansive being.

Continue going through this sequence until you reach zero.

Chapter 5

Create Your Rockstar Team

Create a set of great personal values and surround
yourself with the right people that can form your
support system. Have an optimistic spirit and develop
a strong purpose that you completely believe in and
everything you can imagine is possible for you.
—Andrew Horton

Support systems are comprised of people who genuinely take stock in what you are doing. They care about what choices you are or are not making in life. This support system is made up of a network of friends, family, and peers who also have your back. I remember one of the other entrepreneurs in my mastermind group not too long ago announced that she was selling her business. Me and another person in the group had a difficult time with this, and we quickly started asking questions. What we discovered was that during the seven years of being in her business by way of this mastermind group, supporting, encouraging, giving, and receiving feedback, me and the other business owner realized how much her business was a part of us. We in some regards took ownership of the success or failure of her business. It was really incredible to be a part of this process and to see just how invested we were in her business. This is the level of investment that I'm talking about.

Exploration moment:
What is stopping you from asking for help?_____

_____

_____

_____

_____

_____

_____

_____

_____

_____

_____

_____

_____

_____

_____

_____

_____

Are you willing to let it go? Yes or Yes?

Let's get to it ... because *you deserve* easy and *you deserve* support along this journey of yours!

The universe is an abundant place, and it is waiting for you to just ask for it! What if the universe is ready to give you that which you desire? Understand that the universe is ready, and all you have to do is ask and be willing to receive. Would you ask for it? Would you receive it? If not, why not? Seems easy, right?

I often hear people express complete dread at the idea of asking for help. I am not sure where we get the notion that we are supposed to be, do, and know everything. That is just simply impossible. I commonly hear from clients that they feel that asking for help is seen as a weakness and can leave them feeling even more vulnerable.

Asking for help for anything on any level is completely the opposite of weakness. It demonstrates your awareness and knowledge that you cannot do everything on your own. It takes *a lot of courage* to say, "Yes, I need support and help in XYZ." In doing so, you grow leaps and bounds by:

- Being open to receiving the support you need to take you to the next level in your life
- Gaining an authentic understanding of yourself and your needs
- Discovering new resources to fulfill your needs
- Creating trust and confidence within yourself

Keep in mind that the most inspiring people have learned how to ask others for help. I look up to these individuals because they are invested in themselves. They continue to learn and grow, with the courage to ask for help along the way.

We have to be willing to have the courage to ask others for help, even if we think we may be turned down, and to allow ourselves to be vulnerable like we have never allowed ourselves to be before. No one will support you and your dreams unless you ask for it. In my experience, people are actually honored to help out. They also know the value; they have been helped along their path and see it as a pay-it-forward action.

Giving and Receiving Help

Many people, especially women, feel that we have to give, give, and give and *never* allow ourselves to receive, but here's the secret: energy flows best when we are prepared to both give *and receive*. It is not give, give, give, and it is not a take, take, take either. In order to keep the energy open, there has to be a give *and* a receive element. I give you permission to begin to *receive!* When we allow ourselves to give, we contribute to the world at large. When we receive, we are allowing the world to contribute to us. We allow the energy to flow rather than shut it off.

I love looking at children for guidance on this one. When children really want something, they ask the first person they see, but if they are told no they will often go to the next person in line and ask—and so on until they get what they are looking for, which is a yes. They have not created stories in their heads about being told no. They want it, and they are not stopping until they get the answer that they are looking for. What if we could be in that state while we ask, not allowing our own stories or the stories of others to determine who we are or what we can or cannot create? At what point to do we allow what other people think to take over what is innately ours?

What if in every yes, no, or maybe there was a gift so great it would make asking worth it? What if that gift changed the way you looked at the world and how you showed up to others?

Whatever that just brought up for you, are you willing to let that go? Yes! Now? *Yes!*

Many successful people rely on regular help from personal

or business coaches or mentors. These are trusted guides who help to support them in their dreams. My big secret: I *did not* do this alone. We *cannot* do this alone. So often we think we are less than if we ask for help, that there is something wrong with us. The truth is we are human; we are social beings, and we need relationships. Once you put this into practice, you will *supercharge* your success.

Part of having a support team also means having people on your team to help keep you out of the muck. One important aspect of creating your *rock star* team is to have people on your team who can be there when you lose your flow and fall (even if momentarily).

There's No Need To Go It Alone
We are social beings, and therefore we naturally seek out other people. Humans have one of the most complex social structures on earth, with highly sophisticated methods of communication. We are designed for social interactions, and we find ourselves gathering in families, tribes, communities, and nations.

Something else to consider: energy is always in motion. When we ask for help from others, we allow them to be a contribution to us as we serve in contributing to others, giving and receiving, allowing energy to flow to us and from us in constant motion. We do ourselves and the world a huge disservice when we do not allow for their contributions.

I compare building a support team to having a baseball team. There are some people in the field with you. They get what you are going through. They show up, put in the work, actively supporting you in a positive way. They are the people you have direct access to, and you can call no matter what the hour. This are your star lineup. Then you have the backup team, or the benchwarmers; they are on the team, but they are not the star lineup. They support you as much as they can but often are busy with their own lives (which, by the way, is okay). You know they are there and call on them occasionally when you need them. Then you have the spectators. They come to watch you, and they love to celebrate your successes. They are supportive from a distance, but you know they will always have your back. And finally, you have the people you don't invite to the game. These are the people who don't get you, or maybe they have tried to derail your success, or maybe they are a dream-stealer in your life. These people are better off at home, watching the game on their own televisions. As the coach of your team, you get to choose where people go and what their role will be, if any.

The benefits to building a great team are numerous. Surrounding yourself with people with whom you can share thoughts, ideas, concerns, and goals gives you invaluable feedback, brainstorming, suggestions and advice. Having the right people around you allows you to hear new ideas and learn what has worked without re-creating the wheel.

Additionally, it is easier to discuss tough choices you may have avoided in the past when the people you have surrounded yourself with share your vision and passion. Most importantly, it allows you to share and celebrate your successes with others. It is incredibly inspiring to be surrounded by others who share the same drive and motivation in creating your dream.

Not too long ago I took a long trip out of town, and what

I discovered when I returned was very telling. I had been away from my support team, my resources, and I had decreased the use of my own tools because it was a time to get away and enjoy the people we were visiting.

Upon returning home I had a profound experience. I found myself lost. While I was away and not using my resources, I found that I had taken on the energy of those around me and returned home a completely different person—and not in a positive way. I am pretty sure that I have close friends who are still scratching their heads in puzzlement over the person I temporarily became. It was a foreign feeling to me. I had lost my grounding, my zest for life, and in some ways was completely disconnected from my true self.

I am usually a walking, breathing ball of energy who embraces joy. I have even been accused of being too positive. However, often when we are in the presence of other people we can and do take on their energy. I had made a rookie mistake in not protecting my energy field, and that was when I realized how important the support system is. Days after returning, while I was still in what I felt was a downward spiral, I headed to my mastermind meeting. I faced my support system and got a reality check! It didn't take them long to shut down the story that I was telling myself. Looking back, I am so grateful that they were there to help me recognize that this *was not* me. I won't lie. Initially I felt a little hurt when they were unwilling to support the painful story I was creating. After all, my ego had been front and center, and it took a little hit. I am grateful that I have a support system brave enough to confront me on my own behalf.

What I also realized was that being in the presence of negative people for a long amount of time has the potential to bring anyone down ... even me (the energizer bunny) if I'm not doing the work to protect myself. Let's face it. It is incredibly draining to be in the presence of someone who is always seeing the negative, living with a doom-and-gloom mentality, and trying their hardest to have you join them on their own downward spiral.

Jim Rohn states that, "You are the average of the five people you spend the most time with." Who are you spending your time with? Are they building you up or tearing you down? How are they showing up, positive or negative? What perspective or lens do they see the world through? Doom and gloom or anything is possible?

If like attracts like and you have surrounded yourself with doom and gloomers, how do you think you will turn out? The opposite of that is true as well. If you surround yourself with amazing, dynamic, energetic, and positive people, that is exactly what you will aspire to be. I must say, it is really difficult to play the doom and gloom game when everyone around you thinks you are amazing and asks how they can support your big dreams.

Our energy fields are made up of energy that radiates outward from our bodies, creating an oval shape around us. Our energy extends out approximately a meter to a meter and a half. Keep in mind that we are energy beings, and our energy fields overlap other people's energy fields. You may pick up negative energies when you are in close proximity and absorb their energy. Our energy fields are a reflection of our emotional, spiritual, and thought processes.

It's time to build your team. Here are some questions to ask yourself:

Who currently makes up your team? Do they share in your vision?

_____ ☐Yes ☐No
_____ ☐Yes ☐No
_____ ☐Yes ☐No
_____ ☐Yes ☐No
_____ ☐Yes ☐No
_____ ☐Yes ☐No
_____ ☐Yes ☐No
_____ ☐Yes ☐No
_____ ☐Yes ☐No
_____ ☐Yes ☐No
_____ ☐Yes ☐No
_____ ☐Yes ☐No
_____ ☐Yes ☐No

I must warn you that there is a prerequisite for these individuals on your team. They must hold a positive worldview and an "anything is possible" mindset, along with some cheerleader qualities! Understanding that, let's start creating your team!

The key players for building your *rock star* team

- Family and significant others. You probably already have people in your immediate circle you could recruit to play a more active role in supporting your goals. Get clear on what you would like them to do to support you in your life and professional goals.
- Mentors. These are the people who are doing what you desire to be doing. They have already shown they are successful in turning their dreams into reality; they are ten thousand steps ahead of you. I have been blessed in finding superb mentors who

have been instrumental in supporting me. Contact someone who is an inspiration to you, and explore the idea of having them become your mentor. Consider connecting with them initially for a one-on-one meeting to start forming a relationship. Once that foundation has been established, ask if they would be willing to provide occasional support to you by being available for questions. It's important to be specific about the guidance you are looking for. Be sure to acknowledge and honor their time. I have found people are flattered to be asked to do this and enjoy helping you succeed in your business. They get benefits out of it as well. They end up growing too.

- Accountability partners. Find someone who can hold you accountable for setting your target goals and reaching them. This person is not afraid to give you a swift kick in the rear to get you moving again if or when you lose sight of your target. Being a part of a mastermind group can fill this need as well. This is a great resource for brainstorming ideas and receiving feedback, suggestions, and homework to keep you accountable for following through.

- The compassionate colleagues. These are people on the same level as you in whatever area of life you are in. They are in the trenches with you and should really "get you" and speak your profession's language. When you have a rough day, they understand what you are feeling, as they may have been there before, and can help coach you out of that moment in time.

- The mentee. It has been said one of the best ways for us to learn is to teach someone else. As I mentioned earlier, this is exactly what your mentor gets out of helping you. We all have something to teach someone else; when we give to others, we will receive in other areas of our lives. We may not be a complete expert, but there is always someone that we are ten steps ahead of. Isn't life magical?

What is so amazing about this kind of intentional self-work is that the more you do it, the more you begin attracting people who are aligned with your energy. This helps to draw in the right people you desire on your team. The negative, unsupportive folks will begin to drop off and fade out of your life. Easy, *right*? You automatically start upgrading your circle.

> Keep away from people who try to belittle your ambitions. Small people always do that, but the really great make you feel that you, too, can become great.
> —Mark Twain.

Here are some types of people to watch out for who may be hiding on your support team.

- The Negative Nelly. They have an innate negative lens through which they view the world. They like to find the downside of everything and make certain everyone else is aware of the doom and gloom in the situation or event. There doesn't seem to be anything that pleases them, and they constantly vocalize that "I hate everything!" Because they rarely take ownership over their own lives and behaviors, they find joy in blaming everyone else around them for their misery, which they gladly share with you!
- The Dream Stealers. You may have heard of the crab mentality before. Captured crabs do not require lids on the cages to keep them in because, inevitably,

they pull each other down, never allowing another to reach the top and freedom. Just like crabs, we all have people who will act as dream stealers. In my own experience, dream stealers come in all forms and can even be disguised as someone on your team at first. Dream stealers can be *anyone*, including family, friends, neighbors, coworkers, spouses and significant others. This mentality is best described as "if I can't have it, neither can you." The crabs pull one another down, and, in the end, no one succeeds. If only they knew that by helping their friends they could all achieve freedom from the cage.

- The Energy Drainer. These people simply suck the life out of you. When you walk away from such a person, you may feel like a discombobulated zombie, wondering, What just happened? You feel completely drained. You may even take on some of their low energy or similar characteristics.

- The Toxic Person. These individuals are the master of drama. It doesn't matter what, when, who, where, or why. When they are in your presence you will know it. They like to be the center of attention for all the wrong reasons. It seems to come as second nature, and along with it come negativity, severe judgment, fault finding, and blaming everyone else. When you encounter this person, *run*!

I know we are human, and we are far from perfect beings. What if you are thinking right now, Wow! One of those categories is me or has been me in the past.

I'm glad you are here with me. This is the first step in shifting anything in our lives.

When these people are in your life in some capacity it is up to you to respond to them in ways that protect you and keep you moving forward.

How to handle the types of people mentioned above

- Establish some healthy boundaries. Be aware of your engagement. When you notice a conversation is heading down a negative path, *don't* engage in it!
- Be careful about what you share. If you are sharing your big dreams, that becomes the perfect bait for them to attack, leaving you with only doubts.
- Stay neutral on controversial subjects. If needed, be prepared to politely excuse yourself.
- Limit your contact (if appropriate to do so). If this is an employee or employer, this will need to be addressed differently.
- Protect yourself from taking on other people's energy. Shield yourself by visualizing a white light around your entire body. Think of this as a shield that protects you from any energy that will not be a contribution to you.
- Shift the focus to a more positive light whenever possible.
- Ignore the negative comments, and respond with a more general answer.
- Avoid gossip (gossip can quickly lead to problems). Encourage those participating in gossip to focus more on their own situations and less on pointing a finger at someone else.
- Come from a place of nonjudgment. Often people with negative mentalities are not intentionally trying to cause harm, but have become wrapped up in their own stories.

- Evaluate whether you need to move forward without them on your support team. Often simply spending less and less time with each other does the trick. As your vibration shifts, you will move forward with the people who are at your level.

While I'm teaching these concepts, people will often ask me, "If I have these people in my inner circle right now, how do I go about firing them from my team?"

This is a proactive and very conscious effort. It takes courage to stand up to naysayers and align with your dreams. Do it anyway.

There's never a guarantee that the dark days of life will be forever eliminated, leaving sunny skies and perpetual rainbows. However, when negativity comes creeping into your environment, it is possible to not only mitigate it but completely eliminate it. Keeping the types of relationships that are not working for us is a disservice to both them and us. It does not allow them to grow and does not allow us to grow, and therefore it keeps us both small.

Sometimes people come into our lives and doubt our abilities are meant to be. They somehow strike the chord that gives us the unwavering faith and determination to continue on. So give thanks to those who have helped you carry on.

Michelle Ventor states, "People come into your life for a reason, a season, or a lifetime. When you figure out which it is, you'll know exactly what to do." Not every person who comes into your life will stay with you for the totality of your life's journey. That is the beauty of life. We often attract into our lives those people who serve a purpose for a time. They may teach us a lesson, help us to discover something within us that we have never known, or serve as a catalyst for our change. When relationships begin to die, dwindle, or cease to serve us in a positive way any longer, we often struggle with releasing the relationship. As the tension or drama in the relationship increases, we often begin to question ourselves. "There must be something wrong with me." Instead, realize that sometimes the relationship has served its purpose for both parties and no longer aligns with the needs of the parties involved and their desires.

You will find people who support you and want to see you succeed. It is a powerful thing when you find your tribe. Find the gifts in the experience and in the people. It is okay to let them go for the time being. Who knows? They may appear back in your life when you are ready or they are ready. Sometimes we have to let others go in order to shine brighter. So take a deep breath and, in the kindest way possible, let them go for the time being. There is no easy way to do this, but it is important for you to find a way that will work for you. Here are some suggestions.

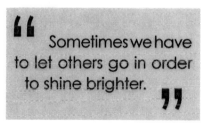

Sometimes we have to let others go in order to shine brighter.

- Express your emotions. Take some time to journal your feelings. Get them out, and take care of yourself.
- Write a letter to them. This can allow for closure (you do *not* need to mail it to them but can if you choose, if it is written in a way that is blameless and kind and you take ownership of your stuff). Remember: this is for closure, not an attempt to

engage with them further or hurt them. Write in a loving, kind, and graceful manner.

- Forgive yourself. Forgive yourself for anything you did to contribute to the issues within the relationship, and allow yourself to forgive them for anything they did, whether they have acknowledged it or not.
- Get support. Be open to receiving support from your support team. This can be an emotional time, but you do not have to go it alone.
- Focus on the here and now. When you do so, you can stop living in the past or the future. Let go of the past. Stop reliving it and creating stories about it. Stay in the present moment.
- Take time for you. Give yourself some distance from the situation or person. Give yourself permission to get a clearer perspective on what has happened. Look for the gifts in it.
- Ownership/Acceptance. Be open to accepting where the relationship began and where it ended. Take ownership for your part, but give the rest to the other person.
- Look inward. Explore who you are and what you desire in life. There are probably many reasons why the relationship did not work out. Learn from the lessons.
- Make a choice. You get to choose who is on your team and who is not. Make the commitment to let them go if they are no longer serving you. This often frees you up from punishing yourself for the reasons the relationship did not work out.

You have worked hard to let go of the people who are no longer serving what you are creating. Once you have designed your *rock star* team, be sure to say two of the most important words in the English language: Thank you.

Maintaining your support system does require some TLC. Showing appreciation will emphasize that you value their support and friendship. Open communication keeps you feeling connected, which demonstrates to them that you are interested in helping and supporting them as well. Create a reciprocal relationship based on both giving and receive. Ensuring that there is a balance between these roles is very important in maintaining a healthy support system.

Not only is it important to find your amazing *rock star* team, but it is also important for us to be a part of other *rock star* teams, so team members can rely on you to stand by their side.

I give you permission to ask for help. Allow yourself to step out of your comfort zone and know that you will be okay. Take your twenty seconds of courage and experience what that "yes!" feels like first hand. Be truly amazed by how much people desire to help you and will actually *thank* you for the opportunity to do so. I also encourage you if you do hear a no to have the courage and grace to say thank you. Continue to ask, and be your amazing self. After all, you are a ten!

Create Your *Rockstar* Team Toolbox

- Identify members of your *rock star* team from within all areas of your life. If some gaps remain, don't sweat it. Find ways to meet new people and ask around to build on what you already have. Try to come up with three to five people in each category.

Family: _____

Friends: _____

Colleagues: _____

Other professionals: _____

Mentors: _____

Accountability partners: _____

Others: _____

- Ask yourself: "What will it take to attract really amazing and dynamic people into my life?" (Access Consciousness)
- EFT Script: See below

EFT Script: Creating a *Rockstar* Team
https://vimeo.com/talkingwithteri/team

To start: Rate yourself on a scale from zero to ten. Ten equals worst; zero equals best. Where would you rate yourself for having your own *rock star* team?

Tap on the karate chop point while saying the following:

- Even though I don't have a true support team, I deeply and completely love and accept myself.
- Even though I have never felt safe asking people to support me, I deeply and completely love and accept myself.
- Even though people in my past have never supported me, I deeply and completely love and accept myself.

Round 1 (Negative Reminder phrase):

	Key:

H: I don't have a strong support system.
EB: I don't trust people to support me. They have always disappointed me.
SE: What if people *do* desire to support me?
UE: What if I've just had the wrong people on my bus?

Key:

H=Head
EB=Eyebrow
SE=Side of eye
UE=Under eye
UN=Under nose
CH=Chin
CB=Collarbone
UA=Under arm

UN: I choose to be open to knowing that there are more possibilities out there for me.
CH: I give myself permission to create my amazing support team.
CB: I am safe in asking for support.
UA: I am so grateful for being open to growth in this area of my life.

Round 2 (Positive phrases):
**Repeat as needed

H: I am open to all the possibilities of creating an amazing support team.

EB: I deserve to be supported, and I allow the universe to support me in every way.

SE: I am safe in creating my amazing life, including my *rock star* team!

UE: I am open to setting boundaries that feel good to me.

UN: I create my reality. I choose to feel supported by amazing people.

CH: I appreciate all the support I receive.

CB: I allow myself to be open to receiving support.

UA: I choose to feel safe and supported.

Continue going through this sequence until you reach zero.

hapter 6

Embrace Gratitude

Acknowledging the good that you already have in
your life is the foundation for all the abundance.
—Eckhart Tolle

The most effective way to shift your vibration from
negative to positive is to practice the art of gratitude.
Gratitude means taking a moment to appreciate what
you are already have and truly seeing your life as the
blessing that it is. You can master the art of gratitude in
the form of a thank you. Appreciation can leave the most
profound impression. Be abundant with your gratitude for
everything and everyone in your life.

What if everything was perfect just the way it is at this very
moment? Even the most challenging difficulties come
into our life to serve a purpose toward our greatest good.
Finding gratitude in even the most difficult moments is a
skill that must be cultivated. It's a process of retraining the
brain to see possibilities versus looking for destruction. With
more practice it becomes second nature. This ability has
allowed me to relax in crisis circumstances and to show
up with more flexibility, playfulness, and much more joy.

It is easy to look back on our lives and point to those

pivotal moments with gratitude that they happened just the way they did. We often realize that if ABC did not happen, XYZ would not have happened as it did either. How can you foster gratitude even when it is all playing out in your life? Is that even possible? Yes! And yes!

When we are able to come from a place of gratitude, we can start to see for the first time in our lives the beauty in every perceived disaster. What if we subconsciously chose the events and circumstances in our lives so we could grow from each of those experiences? What if we chose our parents? What if we chose all the people designated to bringing us to where we stand today? With this thought in mind, I discovered a true gratitude for *all* my life experiences. Without those experiences—the good, the bad, and the ugly—I have no doubt I would not be standing here today. I would not be who I am. Although I once wished that the experiences that shaped me had been different, I understand that everything happened for a reason, and with that I am at peace.

Never in a million years when I was stuck in the muck would I have said, "Yes! Oh, amazing! I'm so grateful!" However, now that I understand why I am here, I can see that it all came together beautifully. I can say, "Yes, I get it!" My heart can forgive the pains of the past and move toward a place of absolute peace that holds a beautiful knowingness toward what lies ahead.

Many authors have spoken about the vibrations of emotions. Scientists have discovered that all emotions include a frequency vibration. It has been said that gratitude and love are the two highest vibrational emotions. Let's tie this to the law of attraction we spoke about earlier. When we are vibrating at the highest vibrational level, we attract at the same level. In some ways, the universe conspires to bring you more of which you desire—like magic! It cannot be any other way. The same is true when we are vibrating at a lower vibrational level.

Being grateful for what you already have is one of the ways to shift your mindset. The more you can stay in this emotional state of being, the more easily and quickly you will be able to generate what you desire in your life. According to Dr. Joe Dispenza in *Evolve Your Brain*, gratitude is the most powerful emotion for increasing your suggestibility. When you bring up the emotion of gratitude, your unconscious body believes that the event has already happened. It also shifts us in a positive way to see more possibilities. When we are grateful, fear disappears, and the abundance we are born with is allowed to shine again in our lives. In many ways, gratitude is responsible for strengthening the faith we hold within ourselves, allowing us to believe in the approaching reality.

Challenge yourself to discover three gifts in every situation, no matter what reality you are experiencing. This allows the brain to shift into a more neutral place and allows you to be in a place to receive all of the possibilities that exist in that moment.

Whenever we are in a place of gratitude, we are sending a subconscious thank you to the universe and asking for more of that. Even better, the abundant universe is ready to supply you with more of it! At a high vibrational level, it is easy to have your RAS search the environment and send you more of that feeling. Life is amazing, isn't it?

Several years ago, my husband and I were riding our bikes along a single dirt track on a popular bike path. I was in the lead, pushing myself and my bike to go faster. Out of nowhere, a huge boulder grew legs and jumped right out in front of me. Having no reaction time, my front tire slammed into the boulder, and I flipped over the handlebars and smashed into the dirt path as I slid to a halt. I picked myself up, dusted myself off, and surveyed the damage. Both of my hands were bleeding, pebbles imbedded in them, and my knee was bleeding through a new hole in my pants. I also had a significantly bruised ego that needed dusting off. As I stood there, my default mode kicked in. I asked myself, "What is the gift in this?" I looked around, searching for the silver lining … and then I found it! Within five inches of where I fell, someone had not cleaned up after their dog. There it was, my gift. I can handle a mangled body, but I know I would not have done so well with *that*! You might say "Sh** happens!" But it is for us to choose what we make of it. I hopped on my bike and continued the ride, laughing.

Getting into the habit of writing what you are grateful for every night is a must-do daily habit. I recommend doing so within the last forty-five minutes of your evening routine because the brain processes things seven times more intensely during this time than any other time of day. So fill that part of the day with yummy goodness, and it will pay off nicely, with dividends. There are an unlimited number of ways to accomplish your gratitude journal, so I will share some examples.

> " Getting into the habit of writing what you are grateful for every night is a must-do daily habit. "

I like to write a list of things that I am grateful for and then end by asking three questions in this format: What would it take for _____ to show up in my life? Others like to write a paragraph detailing one thing they are grateful for, while others like to create lists. There is no wrong way just start.

Examples of Gratitude Lists

I am grateful for:

- My amazing family
- My supportive husband, who puts up with me and my constant energy
- My daughter, who teaches me something every day
- The people whose lives I have the pleasure of impacting
- My courage to try new things out
- Organizations and agencies that book me to speak
- This incredible day and all of its glory
- Our new neighbors, who have been a gift in our lives
- Being of service to others
- Magic erasers
- Freshly picked peaches straight from the tree
- My office neighbor next door for collecting my UPS package and keeping it safe for me

What are some things that you are grateful for lately?

_____
_____
_____
_____
_____
_____
_____
_____
_____
_____
_____
_____

_____

_____

_____

_____

*Now, go purchase a gratitude journal you can write in *every day*! You will love the results!

Become conscious of the things that eat at you. Find the gifts within each of them as well. How we assign meaning to circumstances in our lives is ultimately how we perceive that experience, falling into either the negative or positive category. Observe how we relate those experiences to others based on how we have filed them within our brains. As we share and pass on these stories, we lock them into our subconscious minds, making it easy for us to fall into the victim role if we choose the path of negativity. However, if we choose the path of the victor, we chose the path of positivity. When we reframe events in a more positive light we increase the likelihood of experiencing positive emotions, which allows us to remain in the flow of our lives. This simply helps to shift our thoughts toward more positive, healthy ones that are more in alignment with our true self. Often our most painful times give us the most powerful gifts of our lives. Take a moment to think about a life struggle. Now identify at least three gifts within that struggle.

1). My Struggle _____

The Gifts

- _____
- _____
- _____

2). My Struggle _____

The Gifts

- _____
- _____
- _____

3). My Struggle _____

The Gifts

- _____
- _____
- _____

Another way in which I corporate gratitude into my life is through sharing it with others in the form a thank you card. There is tremendous value to sharing gratitude with the people in my life. Call me an old-fashioned gal, but I still enjoy writing a handwritten note. This exercise serves two purposes: it keeps my gratitude front and center, and those receiving the card feel appreciated and loved. Last year I sent out more than five thousand handwritten cards (based on our printer company's records)! If my speaking audiences are fewer than one hundred people, guess what—they will all get one. I take this very seriously because I truly want to thank the people I have been blessed with coming into their lives. It is amazing to watch how people respond to this small gesture of gratitude. People call me to thank me for my thank you card; others have shouted, "Thank you for your handwritten note" across a crowded event. People love this! Let's face it. When we give thanks, we feel good inside. My love language is gifts, so I get even more of a fabulous feeling when I offer gifts. As a side note, it might be worth looking into figuring out your own love language (which you can do for free at Gary Chapman's www.5lovelanguages.com) to determine how best to meet your needs. Again, you are simply creating more of what you desire. When people ask me the secret to my success, I will always say gratitude, handwritten notes, and follow-up. Most people don't take the time, but this is something I don't skip because I know the value and the power behind it. When I write a note, I write from my heart, and I allow my words to be the conduit for transformation. After all, *words have power.*

My personal gratitude note to you: I am honored and grateful that you have read this book. And here's another *huge* thank you for being bold enough to implement these simple, yet powerful, practices into your life! I am on a mission to create a movement. My goal is to impact more than one million lives with these life-changing principles. I hope I have given you at least one gold nugget that you can take with you on your journey. Many thanks to *you!*

I give you permission to live your life filled with gratitude and allow yourself to embrace life with ease, joy, and glory. Discover the gifts in every situation and become a better person because of it. I also give you permission to be a role model who impacts other people's lives in a positive way. Perhaps you stop, smile, and greet a stranger because you are on a mission to be grateful for your life. Once you give yourself permission to live a life of gratitude, it is impossible not to share your joy with others. I give you permission to embrace your life and all the gifts it has brought to you so far.

I am celebrating where you are, where you have been, and where you are heading. Life is incredible!

Embrace Gratitude Toolbox

Write in your daily gratitude journal in the evening and/ or during the day. Write at least five things that you are grateful for each day. This will allow you to get in touch with what you are grateful for, both personally and professionally. These can be big or small things. Creating a gratitude practice requires daily attention. That is how a habit is created.

Thank You Notes: Create a habit of writing out thank you cards to people. You will be amazed at how great this feels for you and for the lucky recipient.

Find the gifts in every situation, big or small. Look for the silver lining in every situation when you perceive something as negative. It's there, even if you have to dig for it.

Ask Yourself: "What else is possible?" and "How much better can it get?" (Access Consciousness)

EFT Script: Gratitude
https://vimeo.com/talkingwithteri/gratitude

To start: Rate yourself on a scale from zero to ten. Ten equals worst; zero equals best. Where would you rate yourself on your sense of gratitude?

Tap on the karate chop point while saying the following:

- Even though I don't feel that I have anything to be grateful for, I deeply and completely love and accept myself.
- Even though I don't always see the gifts in my life, I deeply and completely love and accept myself.
- Even though it's been challenging for me to see all the positives, I deeply and completely love and accept myself.

Round 1 (Negative Reminder phrases)

H: How can I be grateful when all I see is the negative?
EB: I find myself stuck in the muck.
SE: I tend to complain when things don't go my way.
UE: What if everything is perfect just the way it is?
UN: I choose to know that I have so much to be grateful for.
CH: I give myself permission to see the gifts in every day.
CB: I fill myself with joy, love, and gratitude.
UA: I allow gratitude to fill me.

Key:
H=Head
EB=Eyebrow
SE=Side of eye
UE=Under eye
UN=Under nose
CH=Chin
CB=Collarbone
UA=Under arm

Round 2 (Positive phrases)
**Repeat as needed

H: I am grateful for my life and all the beauty that surrounds me.

EB: I am grateful for the choices I get to make.

SE: I am grateful for all the possibilities that surround me.

UE: I am grateful for change, which brings me growth.

UN: I am grateful for my loved ones.

CH: I am grateful for this amazing place where dreams are created.

CB: I am grateful the magical moments in my life.

UA: I am grateful for my ever-expanding life energy.

Continue going through this sequence until you reach zero.

hapter 7

Celebrate

The more you praise and celebrate your life,
the more there is in life to celebrate.
—Oprah Winfrey

Celebrating what is amazing in our lives is often a lost art. In western culture, celebrating is often perceived as boasting. However, the act of celebrating is the prerequisite for having that which you desire. It starts to put the molecules of the universe in motion for you to create. Researchers have shown that the easiest ways to multiply the positivity you have received from good fortune is to share openly with friends, family, etc. By doing so, everyone wins. Positivity attracts more positivity and inspires others to reach their targets as well. So let's celebrate our personal accomplishments. In almost all team sports, cheerleaders keep the team and their fans motivated, spirited, and feeling alive. This gives the team the confidence to ride the ups and downs of the game.

I get the craziest looks from people for constantly celebrating! I love any reason to celebrate: the day, the weather, my milestones, or anything else that makes me happy at that moment. Celebrating has so many benefits, but for me; it is the fuel that recharges and revives my inspiration. This means celebrating not only huge successes but the tiny ones as well. You are a ten! So let's celebrate you!

I can only imagine how amazing we could all become if we allowed ourselves to celebrate each other's successes. What if we allowed others to succeed? Then their successes could also reflect our loving support? Amazing! Right? Your success is also a success for me, and vice versa. Yes, amazing!

Many people think that celebrating has to be a big production. It doesn't at all. Find what feels good to you. The act of celebrating may look very different from person to person and from situation to situation. Celebrate a job promotion, acceptance letter, overcoming a challenge in your life, or anything else that deserves recognition for what you created and/or went through to get to this place. Celebrate those people in your life you are grateful for. I regularly do a "celebration of friends day" by treating them to coffee, tea, or lunch and sharing with them why they mean so much to me. I typically celebrate any big milestones with many people, while my smaller achievements are noted more privately, with only a few close friends or family. There is no limit to the endless possibilities for celebrating your amazingness!

I remember the first rejection letter I received from large, well-known publishing company. I opened the letter and read it; a profound sense of joy rushed over me. I remember saying, "They actually responded!" I had sent out at least thirty, and was the first response … six months later. I was so delighted! Yes, I wish it would have been an acceptance letter, but I was just as content. I immediately called my husband to go celebrate! In a sense, I was celebrating the work I had put into it.

Keep in mind that not every celebration is about success or monetary gain. We can celebrate our failures if we see them as an opportunity for growth. When we allow ourselves to be in that vibration, we are also utilizing the law of attraction in our favor. When I bought or received a fancy candle I found myself saving it instead of waiting for a special occasion. Then I realized life is my special occasion, so now I burn them with gratitude and an abundance mindset, knowing there will always be more. By the same token, I now find everyday uses for my champagne glasses. Milk tastes delightful in a champagne glass, water tastes scrumptious in a wine glass, and orange juice tastes incredible in a margarita glass! I could go on, but you get the point.

Through celebrating we give the universe a subconscious thank you, which activates the RAS in the brain. Guess what? You are reinforcing it, and naturally the universe will try to give you more of that!

Celebrating the smallest and most mundane aspects of our lives can transform; being happy can create more abundance in your life. Intentions can be *fun* and make life more extraordinary. Therefore, you are able to draw more experiences into your life. See how this all works?

This is the new evidence. If you would like more things to celebrate, simply say, "I'll take more of that!" (Access Consciousness). The evidence is all around us, and we have to be open to seeing all the possibilities come alive.

It is not your job to figure out how it's all going to work

out. Your job is to keep faith that it will work out, in its own perfect way. Then find gratitude and celebrate. I wish someone had told me this twenty years ago! I am a self-proclaimed type A personality who loves nothing more than getting things figured out. Are you telling me that I can let go and allow it to all play out without having to control it? #Boom.

I give you permission to *celebrate* just being you, to acknowledge your successes and all the beautiful and unique characteristics that make up *you*. Celebrate other people's accomplishments. I give you permission to call some friends, make a plan, and get yourself in a place of gratitude for the risks that you and those around you have taken, the successes you have created, and the possibilities for what is yet to come! *You are amazing!*

Celebrate Toolbox

Daily celebration of self. Discover one thing every day to celebrate you. As mentioned earlier, you are a ten on the scale of one to ten every day! So let's start there.

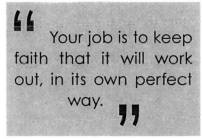
" Your job is to keep faith that it will work out, in its own perfect way. "

Ask yourself: "How much better can it get?"(Access Consciousness).

EFT Script: Celebrate
https://vimeo.com/talkingwithteri/celebrate

Rate yourself on a scale from zero to ten. Ten equals worst; zero equals best. Where would you rate yourself on celebrating your successes (big or small) in life?

Tap on the karate chop point while saying the following:

- Even though I rarely celebrate anything, I deeply and completely love and accept myself.
- Even though I'm not sure I have anything to celebrate in my life, I deeply and completely love and accept myself.
- Even though I'm afraid people will think I am a show-off if I celebrate my successes, I deeply and completely love and accept myself.

Round 1 (Negative Reminder phrases)

H: I have nothing to celebrate.
EB: People will think I'm weird if I celebrate my successes.
SE: I couldn't possibly celebrate me! That would be silly.
UE: I like to celebrate others ... which is a part of this too.
UN: What if celebrating allowed for more things to celebrate? That would be amazing!
CH: I give myself permission to celebrate my life and all of its amazingness! Wahoo!
CB: I am safe to celebrate.
UA: I allow myself to celebrate starting *now*.

Key:

H=Head
EB=Eyebrow
SE=Side of eye
UE=Under eye
UN=Under nose
CH=Chin
CB=Collarbone
UA=Under arm

Round 2 (Positive phrases)
**Repeat as needed

H: I fill myself with reasons to celebrate my life.

EB: Life is amazing, and I choose to have more of that to celebrate!

SE: I choose to create a magical life.

UE: I allow celebrations to happen all around me.

UN: I support others in their dream creation as well as me in my own. Let's celebrate!

CH: I am safe.

CB: I give myself permission to celebrate the gifts in my life and all my successes.

UA: I allow myself to give and receive amazingness into my life. Life is delicious!

Continue going through this sequence until you reach zero.

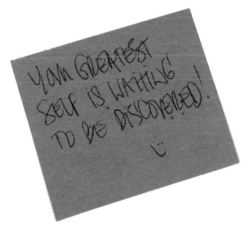

hapter 8

Inspired Action

If you don't go after what you want, you'll never have it.
If you don't ask, the answer is always no.
If you don't step forward, you're
always in the same place.
—Nora Roberts

Many of us know what we want but have never taken the time to create a plan, set targets, and finally take action to set them in motion. I use the term *inspired action*—inspired because as you work toward a target, work toward your heart's passion, you will get excited and jazzed about the possibilities that each day brings to you. Your excitement will impact others with whom you come into contact. What a win-win-win situation! We spend too much time playing with an idea, giving excuses, and staying stuck in the exact same place as when we started. Just get in the practice of taking the next step, and you win the momentum to keep going.

For those of you who struggle with the barrier of perfectionism, try for 90 percent. You will be amazed at how shifting that mindset helps you let go of the need to get it perfect.

In his book *Your Right to Be Rich*, Napoleon Hill calls this concept *personal initiative*. According to Hill, personal initiative is a vital principle in achieving success. To take personal initiative, however, we must first establish a strong and clear purpose, a target that we can focus on and diligently work toward. I purposefully use the word *target* instead of the word *goal* for a reason. A target is a direction to aim for. However, it also allows us to remain open in case something even better shows up.

While many people have a very clear idea of what their targets are and how to accomplish them, others are unclear about what they would like to do in life and therefore have never defined their targets in order to take inspired action. This is a primary difference between those who achieve success and those who do not. A longitudinal study done at Harvard years ago found a striking difference between successful and unsuccessful people. The common denominator in those who had achieved success was that they had carefully identified what their specific targets were and had written them down. As simple as this sounds, it is a powerful tool and a vital step in accomplishing any major life target.

Recipe for Success
The process of searching introspectively for the most meaningful and rewarding actions you can take in your life, defining those thoughts and feelings into simple targets, and focusing wholeheartedly on their completion is the recipe that allows your dreams to take flight. This recipe effectively focuses your attention toward what you desire and empowers you to create positive change in the direction you are in charge of creating. Another vital element in this process is establishing a routine of self-discipline.

My husband can attest that I have often been a master of

distraction, spreading my energy in a variety of directions rather than focusing completely on one target at a time. My high-energy personality tends to default to this tendency, which has led me to establish my daily intentions planner for taking inspired action toward my targets. These vary each day as I look at what needs to be completed for that week. As an example, targets may include making certain phone calls, scheduling appointments, creating a new document, researching, working on my journals for publishing, etc. I consider these the tasks that require attention to be completed so that other things can fall into place easily. This more or less equates to building time into my routine to focus on my targets. Self-discipline is required because there are always other things that I could be doing.

Peter Shepherd stated, "Action is where it's at as far as making dreams come true. We ourselves are the prime channel for our creations, so if we don't act but just wait, then we are blocking the channel. If we do act then we will be supported by all that we are connected to ... which is *all* that is if we act with love and service as our motivation." The RAS, as we talked about earlier, is also impacted, finding more and more evidence in your world to support your targets.

So often we live in a wait-and-see world—wait to see if someone else takes action on our thoughts, ideas, plans, and dreams. What if you took action first? What amazing possibilities are you ready to take action on *now*? What amazing possibilities are you ready to take action on *now*?

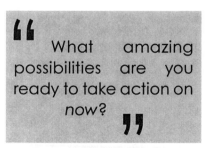

> What amazing possibilities are you ready to take action on *now*?

Inspired action

- Explore and identify what brings you joy. Delve into the areas of life that you love and that brings you the most personal gratification. Weed through ideas until you have a tangible goal you feel excited about and ready to achieve. Write it down and post it where you can view it daily. The simple act of writing it down will put you ahead of the majority.

  _____

  _____

  _____

  _____

  _____

  _____

  _____

  _____

  _____

  _____

- Use tools to help remind you of the target you are working toward. Create a Vision Board, a popular and useful tool, a visual representation of your targets. Compile words, pictures, or other images onto a poster board to represent the things and experiences to be, do, or have in your life. Encourage yourself to step out of your comfort zone and play with your creativity during this process. Hang the board somewhere nearby and look at it daily to give you a constant reminder of where you will soon be in your life. The most important element is to act *as if* you have already created this in your life. As one of the legends in this metaphysical work, Nevel Goddard, said, "Make your future dream a present fact by assuming the feeling of the wish fulfilled."

- Create an accountability process that keeps you engaged, inspired, and on track for success. This could mean joining forces with a friend, spouse, or mastermind group to gain support and remind you of what you are working toward.
- Make conscious choices rather than heeding obligations or replaying in your mind what you "should" be doing. Consciously choosing your actions will make you feel empowered and excited about the things you are doing.
- Reward yourself! We all have tasks we don't like to do, but we know that at the end of the day they have to get done somehow. Reward yourself with a fun project, time with your family, a bike ride—whatever you are passionate about.

I give you permission to take inspired action to set your life in motion! Dream *big*, play, be inspired, live out loud. No matter what you call it, it is now time for you to *do* the things you have been waiting to do. Be an inspiration to others, a contribution to this amazing world, and leave your legacy starting *today*! I am here to celebrate the best parts of you. I can inspire you and motivate you, but it is up to you take inspired action! I believe in you!

Inspired Action Toolbox
Daily Intentions Planner. This is a powerful tool I created for my own life to help me stay organized and focused on my daily targets. I use this technique to reflect both my personal and professional life. (See Appendix D.)

To order your own copy of our Daily Intentions Planner go to www.talkingwithteri.com.

Ask yourself: "What great thing can I create and generate now?" (Access Consciousness).

EFT: Taking Inspired Action
https://vimeo.com/talkingwithteri/action

To start: Rate yourself on a scale from zero to ten. Ten equals worst; zero equals best. Where would you rate yourself on taking action?

Tap on the karate chop point while saying the following:

- Even though I keep myself from taking action for my own fear of standing out, I deeply and completely love and accept myself.
- Even though I am stepping out of my comfort zone to follow my dreams, I deeply and completely love and accept myself.
- Even though it's hard for me to imagine what it would be like to follow through on my dreams and desires, I deeply and completely love and accept myself.

Round 1 (Negative Reminder phrases)

H: I'm afraid to stand out and show the world ... *me.*

EB: It's easy to shrink to fit in, so why should I take action?

SE: What if I took action on my dreams and desires?

UE: What if they all turned out better than I ever imagined?

UN: What if that means stepping out of my comfort zone to experience more joy?

CH: I could do that. No I couldn't. Yes I can. Yes! Yes, I can!

CB: I realize that by not taking action I remain stuck.

Key:

H=Head
EB=Eyebrow
SE=Side of eye
UE=Under eye
UN=Under nose
CH=Chin
CB=Collarbone
UA=Under arm

UA: I choose to be open to all the amazing possibilities that surround me.

Round 2 (Positive phrases)
**Repeat as needed

H: I am open to creating a plan to take more action and follow through on my goals.
EB: I am choosing to take a baby step each and every day!
SE: I choose happiness for me.
UE: I am grateful for the action I have taken so far.
CH: I am here and taking inspired action *now*.
CB: I am *rocking* my life! Wahoo!
UA: Each day that I expand into myself, I allow others to do the same!

Continue going through this sequence until you reach zero.

$\mathscr{C}$hapter 9

Practice Everyday

Be the change you wish to see in the world.
—Mahatma Gandi

I used to think that once I worked on myself and got myself clear of all my baggage I would be free and clear for good. The truth is we all have stuff that comes up in our everyday lives. We *all* require our own work, constantly.

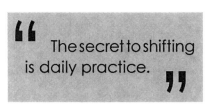
> The secret to shifting is daily practice.

The secret to shifting is daily practice. Our brains have been programed to be in the default mode. Shifting takes time, but *it is possible*. Our brains require us to overlearn a new skill in order to become proficient in it. In other words, it took us many years to cement today's habitual patterns and thought processes. I think it is safe to say that it will require some practice to shift that paradigm. Talking value in daily personal growth allows us to become who we were meant to be. As with any skill we learn, whether we are playing a new sport or learning how to play the guitar, our brains require repetition in order to master it.

It takes approximately thirty days to make a change,

sixty days to make it a routine, and ninety days to create a permanent habit. This change takes *practice*. When we practice, we begin creating new neurological pathways in the brain. When we create new practices with these tools, we start shifting into a new way of living. Practice allows us to stay on our game when life throws us surprises. We are able to take care of ourselves on a daily basis. And we are able to stay out of the muck for longer periods of time.

I confess ... I am not one for patience. I am one of those people who think I can pick up a golf club for the first time and be the next up and coming pro golfer without even a practice shot. So I get the struggle over having to practice and be patient. Practice-smactice ... I am in the same boat. I get it. So psst ..., let's do this practice thing together!

What happens for most clients is they will reach a place where they oscillate between both of these worlds until they get to a point where the shift pushes them over to the other side. Then they think, act, and become more and more a part of a new mindset.

"Teri, this sounds great and all, but I just don't have enough time to spend on myself. After all, I have my children to take care of, after school activities to attend to, dinner to cook, laundry to fold, a house to clean, bills to pay, and the dog to walk. I *have no time*."

Here is the funny thing about that ... Don't kick me when I say this, but that is just an excuse for not taking care of *you*.

In his book *The Magic of Thinking Big*, author David

Schwartz coined the phrase *excusitis*, or the disease of failures. The number one all too common excusitis phrase is, "I don't have time." According to Schwartz, we all have time if we learn the best way to apportion it. In his book, Schwartz illustrates a typical one-week allocation of time. I appreciate his insight because I think it gives real evidence that we *do* have plenty of time to get things accomplished.

> 24 hours/day=168 hrs/wk
> 50 hrs/wk at work +commuting time
> <u>51 hrs/wk sleeping</u>
> =101 hrs/wk
> <u>15 hrs/wk eating</u>
> =116 hr/wk
> <u>24 hrs relaxing, reading, kids, exercise</u>
> =140 total
> <u>4 hrs/wk community/church</u>
> =144 hrs/wk
> 168 hrs minus144 hrs equals 24 hours left in the week

According to Schwartz, twenty-four hours in the week are unaccounted for. So the question is, what are you doing with your time? Schwartz argues that the phrase "I don't have time" is the alibi many give for mediocrity, which ultimately leads to failure. Do we really not have the time, or are we just blind to time killers holding us back from our full potential?

The most common of the time killers are television, social media, and video gaming. According to Nielsen statistics, the average American over the age of two years spends more than thirty-four hours per week watching live television, plus another three to six hours watching taped programs.

Nielsen's annual social media report states that in 2016, Generation X (ages thirty-five to forty-nine) spent thirty-two hours on all forms of media. They were followed by millennials (ages eighteen to thirty-four) with twenty-six hours per week. Then came baby boomers (ages fifty to sixty-seven) with twenty hours per week. According to Facebook's website statistics, in March 2016 Facebook alone had 1.28 billion daily active users and 1.94 billion monthly active users.

I hope the connection is evident here. Saying "I don't have time" but potentially spending a significant portion of time on television and social media doesn't quite mesh. So what are you willing to change, shift, or rearrange to give up the excuse of having no time? You are the only person allocating your time. Whether it's for your business, or for personal reasons, can you commit to making more productive use of your hours in the day?

Creating a practice in anything means finding what works for you and creating a habit or routine for it on a daily basis. It also involves trusting the process and allowing teachers, mentors, coaches, etc., to show up in your life. So many of my teachers have seemed to have been magically orchestrated, which makes sense when we remember that are usually introduced to things, people and circumstances when we are ready for the lessons they are here to teach. Which means that whether you bought this book for yourself or someone else gave it to you, you were ready to hear its message.

Also understand as you fill your bag with tools that some

may be better suited for certain circumstances than others. Start with the basics, and change and add to as you see fit.

I am a consistent student of learning, filling my mind with new knowledge every day. A great philosopher, Sir Francis Bacon, once said, "Knowledge is power." This is true not just for some of us but for all of us. Whether it is books, CDs, lectures, workshops, conferences, articles, pod casts, etc., there is an abundance of knowledge out there, and it is yours for the taking.

Seeking out and absorbing this information is very important to personal growth. However, even more critical to growth is the art of implementation. We have all been there, myself included. You attend a workshop or training or read a book, and when it's over, the information gets filed away or, worse, forgotten and never allowed to be applied to your life or become an asset to you.

I used to think I could implement the tools I have acquired once or twice, reach my targets, and be done. Wrong! I was so wrong. I realize it still requires everyday practice to maintain what I am creating.

In fact, to this day, I still practice these principles daily. Take a peek at Appendix E for how I create my day! They may be overdone, but I know that I will always maintain a practice of taking care of myself from this energetic perspective. I plan to continue this practice because it is the responsible party for getting me to this stage in my life, doing so with much joy and gratitude. Plus there is a side benefit; it feels great to practice these techniques!

I have acquired many tools and concepts and

implemented them into my everyday practice. Trust me—I would not share things that did not work. Many people have thanked me for sharing these tools, and I have been lucky enough to witness firsthand how powerful they can be in reclaiming personal power.

We are all a work in progress. Even now, I have some moments. Even though they are few and far between, I know exactly what to do. In those moments, I stop … and remind myself to shift. I am in perpetual practice mode. I encourage you to adopt the tools within these pages, make them your own, and practice them with fervor. Practice them daily, and be open to seeing the shift happen before your eyes.

We are human beings, which means we are always growing, changing, and moving, just like the world around us. You have shown that you are ready to take ownership of your own life and your own happiness. Congratulations! By the way, how will you be celebrating this success?

I give you permission to create a daily practice of placing *you* front and center in your life! Be your best self. Create a daily practice that is designed to place you on the path of your dreams. You deserve to live your life to the fullest, to have people question how you can be so happy, and to step into the person you have always known but feared. You are here for a bigger purpose. I encourage you to reach out to others and help guide them on the path to success. As you live your life joyfully, you will automatically give permission to others to do the same. Be all of you!

hapter 10

Be the Magic of You!

The difference between ordinary and
extraordinary is that little extra.
—Jimmy Johnson

Welcome to the final chapter in this book and the first chapter in all the possibilities of the life you choose! If you have truly implemented the tools within these pages, you will notice the shifts that have shown up in your life. Once you have played with these tools and feel that you have created a daily routine, take a few minutes to fill out the questionnaire that you filled at the beginning. What do you notice? What's showing up differently?

We started on this journey together looking at how you can own your happiness and take full responsibility for your life in every aspect and make the choice to be more. Then we looked at how to eliminate your head trash to get out of your self-sabotaging tendencies and take control of what you are creating in your world. Next, we played with the idea of stepping outside your comfort zone to discover the possibilities beyond your own limitations. We didn't stop there. We explored who you have in your support system and how to create your *rock star* team to contribute to what you are creating. We embraced gratitude by uncovering the gifts and seeing experiences happening for us, not to us. We explored the importance the act of celebration in every aspect of our lives. We learned the power in taking inspired action to set our dreams in motion. And finally, we discovered how everyday practice can be key to creating total transformation in your life. It is your time to live your extraordinary!

The tools in each of these sections were designed to help you expand and be more of who you are already are. Now it is your time to shine. You get to choose what you do next. Will you incorporate these or choose to do nothing at all? Either way, I wish you massive success in creating the life that you fall in love with, waking up each morning wondering how much better it can get.

During a training I attended with Jack Canfield, he shared a story about the Golden Buddha. The story goes like this. In 1957, monks in Bangkok, Thailand, were in the process of moving a large clay Buddha from one location to a new location. During the move, the Buddha slipped, and some of the plaster coating cracked. The monk in charge of the move was clearly distraught over what had happened. He threw a tarp over the Buddha to keep it dry. That night he went out to check on it. As he shined a flashlight on it, he noticed something shining back. After further investigation, they discovered the Buddha, standing almost ten feet tall, weighing five and a half tons,was made of solid gold, with a net worth of $250 million.

The theory is that the monks had heard that the Burmese were planning to invade Thailand. The monks had taken precautions and covered the Golden Buddha with clay and painted it to make it look worthless to prevent it from being stolen. All of the monks had been massacred in the war, and there were no survivors to reveal that they had the Golden Buddha. The true identity had been forgotten for almost two hundred hundred years.

Think about the word "dis-cover": we remove the cover from what was already there. Like the Golden Buddha, we too have gone through life covered up with clay. In some ways, we put the clay there to protect ourselves, but the majority of the time it has been put there by someone else. The clay represents all our fears, doubts, worries, judgments, insecurities, etc.—all the stuff that blocks our brilliance from truly shining. Our brilliance is meant to shine brightly. We all have so many unique gifts and talents, plus a sense of wonder, to be acknowledged. We all have a Golden Buddha within waiting to be discovered. Your time to shine is *now*! The tools in this book are designed for just that: to "dis-cover" what you already have within and chip away any clay that no longer serves you! Be the magic of you!

As we part, I ask, "What will you choose today? Tomorrow? And the days, months, and years to follow?"

Remember. You are more powerful than you allow yourself to be. Let's do this together. The late Dr. Wayne Dyer urged in a conference I attended, "Don't die with your music still in you. You are here to play your music." Some of the most extraordinary moments can come from very ordinary moments. Those are the defining moments in life, and it is up to us to determine how we respond to those moments.

You have the choice to discover the magic within and truly live your life extraordinary! When I leave this life, I desire to have it inscribed on my gravestone that I loved passionately, learned passionately, inspired passionately, and lived passionately. What will your legacy be? You are limitless, powerful, and amazing. May you live extraordinary and inspire others to do the same.

As a therapist, I have used the metaphor of peeling back the layers of the onion on numerous occasions. However, in more recent years I use this metaphor with a twist, thanks to an incredible healing friend, Dr. Hemerson, who has become a guide to me in my life and offers wisdom when I most need it. Have you ever wondered what is really inside an onion?

It is something we are all in search of ...

When we peel back all of the layers of the onion, what you find is ... self-love. In order for us to move forward in our lives and to own our happiness, we must fully embrace, accept, and love the beautiful beings we are, unconditionally. It begins with us. As we do so, we can give from our surplus. We were brought into this world as precious beings, and our lives were designed to be lived fully! Let's do this!

My Letter to You

Dear Amazing,

There will always be someone who is prettier, smarter, funnier than you. *Don't compare yourself.* You are unique, and that is what makes you one-of-a-kind, special, and lovable. You are the best person that you can be! *Embrace yourself!*

There will always be someone who doesn't understand you or get you. Know that *you are still okay.* You *will not* please everyone, so don't break your spirit trying.

There will always be a time when you beat yourself up, wishing the situation had worked out differently, that you had responded versus reacted, or just had a different attitude about it. *Forgive yourself.*

There will always be a time when you want the memories to go away; you might even find yourself in old patterns that no longer serve you. *Stay strong.* This time, too, will pass.

There will always be a time when you lose your words and will not know what to say. *Find your voice.* You are important, and you have an important message to share with those who support your growth. *Share your voice.*

There will always be someone who has less than you. *Be kind to them.* You do not know the path they have traveled. Be the one to show them what true friendship looks like.

There will always be times you are filled with a sense of pride, thinking to yourself, "Yes! I did it!" *Pat yourself on the back!* And pause ... pause in that moment, and breathe it all in.

There will always be your inner voice encouraging you and cheering you on as you look fear in the face. *Follow your heart.*

There will always be someone who builds you up, says kind words about you, and sees you for the truly amazing person you are. *Believe them.* They have been brought into your life for a reason. Do not negate what they see in you, which you may not be able to see in yourself—yet. They are still telling the truth. Believe them, until you are able to believe it yourself.

I give you permission today to live your life with purpose, passion, and some playfulness. You deserve the best! You deserve to experience happiness in its truest forms.

I am so proud of you for the courage you have shown in stepping outside your comfort level, for being vulnerable as you allow others to support you in the healing process, for not having it all figured out, and being open to all the possibilities.

Be a part of the movement that inspires people, young and old, to live their lives to the fullest, to achieve their wildest dreams, and to believe in the value of themselves. *Be your amazing!*

I wish for you to know that joy is to be lived, by you and through you, that greatness lives in *all of us*, not just some of us, that you get to choose your life story. Amazing things can and do happen. When you start living your life with happiness, you automatically give permission to others to do the same. You are the creator of your reality. Fill your life with positive people who inspire you to learn and grow and allow you to succeed!

Be the Magic of You

To get a free download of this letter go to: <u>www. TalkingWithTeri.com</u>

PS I would love to connect with you. If you have found this book to be of benefit, please don't hesitate to contact me with your success story. You are shaping not only yourself but every single person you come in contact with! I am so proud of you and the journey you have taken. Let's s keep this momentum going. Join me at <u>www.talkingwithteri.com</u> for the next adventure in you!

Talking With Teri
6021 S. Syracuse Way, Suite #216
Greenwood Village, CO 80111

References

Brene, B. (2012). *Daring Greatly: How the Courage to Be Vulnerable Transforms the Way We Live, Love, Parent, and Lead.* New York, NY: Gotham Books.

Brene, B. (2010). *The Gifts of Imperfection: Let Go of Who You Think You're Supposed To Be and Embrace Who You Are.* Center City, MN: Hazeldon.

Casey, S. (2017, July 1). The 2016 Nielsen Social Media Report. Retrieved July 17, 2017, from http://www.nielsen.com/us/en/insights/reports/2017/2016-nielsen-social-media-report.html

Craig, G. (1995). "What is EFT or Tapping?" Retrieved August 31, 2014, from http://www.emofree.com

Dispenza, J. (2007). *Evolve Your Brain.* Deerfield Beach, FL: Health Communications, Inc.

Dispenza, J. (2014). *You Are the Placebo: Making Your Mind Matter.* Carlsbad, CA: Hay House.

Douglas, G. and Heer, D. (1990) "Access Consciousness and the Greatness of You." Retrieved May 20, 2015, from www.accessconsciousness.com

Dyer, W. W. (2014, March 28). *Keynote*. Lecture presented at I Can Do It Conference, Colorado Convention Center, Denver.

Emoto, M. (2010). "What is the Photograph of Frozen Water Crystals?" Retrieved April 2, 2014, from <u>www.masaru-emoto.net</u>

Facebook. (2017). Retrieved July 17, 2017, from <u>https://newsroom.fb.com/company-info/</u>

Hawkins, D. R. (2013). *Power versus Force: The Hidden Determination of Human Behavior*. Carlsbad, CA: Hay House.

Harvard Mental Health Letter, "Children's Fears and Anxieties," Dec. 2004, Vol 21, No. 6, PP 1–4.

Hinckley, D. (2012). Nielsen's Annual Social Media Report. Retrieved May 12, 2014, from <u>http://www.nydailynews.com/entertainment/tv-movies/americans-spend-34-hours-week-watching-tv-nielsen-numbers-article-1.1162285#ixzz2YZjqlvzk</u>

Ipsos Open Thinking Exchange (IOT). Retrieved May 12, 2014, from <u>www.ipsos-na.com</u>

Losier, M, J. (2006). *Law of Attraction: The Science of Attracting More of What You Want and Less of What You Don't*. New York, NY: Wellness Central.

Lyubomirsky, S. (2008) *The How of Happiness: A New Approach to Getting the Life You Want*. New York, NY: Penguin Books.

Mishra, A. (2009). 'Positivity, by Barbara L. Fredriskson',

Journal of Positive Psychology, 4(6), 578–580. Doi:10.1080/17439760903157109

Maxwell, M. (2015). *Psycho-Cybernetics.* New York, NY: TarcherPerigee.

Peiffer, V. (2001). *Positively Fearless: Breaking Free of the Fears That Hold You Back.* Hammersmith, London: Thorsons.

Schwartz, D. (2014). *The Magic of Thinking Big.* New York, NY: Penguin Books.

Recommended Books

A., Hicks, E., & Hicks, J. (2009). *Ask and It Is Given: Learning To Manifest Your Dreams*, Carlsbad, CA: Hay House, Inc.

Brown, B. (2015). *Daring Greatly: How the Courage to Be Vulnerable Transforms The Way We Live, Love, Parent, and Lead.* New York, NY: Gotham Books.

Brown, B. (2010). *The Gifts of Imperfection: Let Go of Who You Think You're Supposed To Be and Embrace Who You Are.* Charleston, SC: Hazeldon.

Burg, B. & Mann, J. D (2015) *The Go-Giver: A Little Story About a Powerful Business Idea.* London: Portfolio Penguin.

Canfield, J., & Hansen, M. V. (1996). *The Aladdin Factor: How To Ask For and Get Anything You Want In Life.* USA: Time Warner International.

Canfield, J., & Switzer, J. (2015). *The Success Principles: How to Get From Where You Are To Where You Want To Be.* New York: William Morrow.

Chopra, D. (2009). *The Seven Spiritual Laws of Success: A Practical Guide To the Fulfillment of Your Dreams.* London: Bantam

Covey, S. R. (2013). *The Seven Habits of Highly Effective People: Powerful Lessons in Personal Change.* New York: Simon & Schuster.

Dyer, W. W. (2004). *The Power of Intention: Learning To Co-Create Your World Your Way.* Carlsbad, CA: Hay House.

Dyer, W. W. (2013) *Wishes Fulfilled: Mastering the Art of Manifesting.* Carlsbad, CA: Hay House.

Eden, D. (1998) *Energy Medicine.* NY, NY: Penguin Putman.

Emoto, E., (2005). *The Hidden Messages in Water.* New York: Atria Books.

Gawain, S. (2002). *Creative Visualization: Use the Power of Your Imagination to Create What You Want in Your Life.* New World Library.

Hawkins, D. R. (2002). *Power Versus Force: The Hidden Determinants of Human Behavior.* Carlsbad, CA: Hay House.

Hay, L. (2008). *You Can Heal Your Life.* Australia: Hay House, Inc.

Hill, N. & Sartwell, M. (2007). *Napoleon Hill's Keys to Success: The Seventeen Principles of Personal Achievement.* New York: Plume.

Hill, N. & Stone, C. (1997). *Success Through a Positive Mental Attitude.* Englewood Cliffs, N.J.: Prentice-Hall.

Hill, N. (1960). *Think and Grow Rich.* New York: Fawcett Crest Books.

Jeffers, S. (2017). *Feel the Fear and Do It Anyway.* S.I: Vermilion.

Losier, M. J. (2007). *Law of Attraction: The Science of Attracting More of What You Want and Less of What You Don't*. New York: Wellness Central.

Maltz, M (1960). *Psycho-Cybernetics: A New Way to Get More Living Out of Life*. Englewood Cliffs, NJ: Prentice-Hall.

Ray, J. A. (2006). *The Science of Success: How to Attract Prosperity and Creative Life Balance Through Proven Principles*. Carlsbad, CA: SunArk Press.

Robbins, A. (1992). *Awaken the Giant Within: How to Take Immediate Control of Your Mental, Emotional, Physical and Financial Destiny!* Free Press.

Robbins, A. (2015). *Unlimited Power: The New Science of Personal Achievement*. New York: Simon & Schuster.

Ruiz, M., & Wilton, N. (2012). *The Four Agreements: A Practical Guide to Personal Freedom*. San Rafael, CA: Amber-Allen.

Schwartz, D. (2016). *The Magic of Thinking Big*. London: Vermilion.

Tolle, E. (2008). *The Power of Now: A Guide to Spiritual Enlightenment*. Sydney: Hachette Australia.

Other great inspiration tools for you to enjoy:
Notes From the Universe. © www.tut.com.®

Sign up to receive free e-mails from the Universe that incorporate your goals for the year. This is a daily must for inspiration, with a fun new perspective that inspires you to see your role in the massive universe.

*A*ppendix A

The Clearing Statement in Action, with Gary Douglas and Dr. Dain Heer

As I mentioned earlier, this clearing statement is a tool pulled from Access Consciousness. This tool is designed to bring up the energies of the things that block us from creating more of the things we desire. Your point of view creates your reality, which is responsible for what shows up in our reality. Using this statement helps to destroy the limitation you are creating, allowing you to function from a more conscious state of being. In doing so, you shift the energy from an unconscious state, to get you unstuck from the muck! The best part is you don't have to understand it for it to work.

The clearing statement: "Right and wrong, good and bad, POD, POC, all nine, shorts, boys, and beyonds."

Use it for any limitation, judgment, etc., that is limiting you from being your extraordinary self.

As we would ask in Access consciousness, anything that, that brings up for you times a billion god zillion, billion god zillion, billion god zillion, are you willing to revoke, destroy, uncreate all of that? [Yes.]

"Right and wrong, good and bad, POD, POC, all nine, shorts, boys, and beyonds."

Explanation of Clearing Statement

Right and wrong, good and bad: what's good, perfect and correct about this?

What's wrong, mean, vicious, terrible, bad, and awful about this?

What's right and wrong, good and bad?

POD
The point of destruction immediately following whatever you decided. It's like pulling the bottom card from of a house of cards. The whole thing falls down.

POC
The point of creation of the thoughts, feelings, and emotions immediately preceding whatever you decided.

All Nine
Stands for nine layers of crap that we're taking out. Somewhere in those nine layers, there's got to be a pony, because you couldn't put that much crap in one place without having a pony in there. It's crap you're generating yourself, which is the bad part. The good part is that because you created it, you can change it.

Shorts
The short version of: What's meaningful about this? What's meaningless about this? What's the punishment for this? What's the reward for this?

Boys

Stands for nucleated spheres. Have you ever been told you have to peel the layers of the onion to get to the core of an issue? Well, this is it—except it's not an onion. It's an energetic structure that looks like one. These are preverbal. Have you ever seen one of those kids' bubble pipes? Blow here and create a mass of bubbles at the other end of the pipe? As you pop one bubble, it fills back in. Basically, these have to do with those areas of life where we've continuously tried to change something, with no affect. This is what keeps something repeating ad infinitum …

Beyonds

Feelings or sensations that stop your heart, stop your breath, or stop your willingness to look at possibilities. It's like when your business is in the red and you get another final notice; you say, "Argh!" You weren't expecting that right now.

The beauty, magic, and potency of the Access Consciousness Clearing Statement is its capacity to clear the hidden stuff that you aren't even aware of that keeps you stuck!

$\mathcal{A}$ppendix B

Step-by-Step Instructions for Emotional
Freedom Technique (EFT)
https://vimeo.com/talkingwithteri/whatiseft

I will walk you through the Basic Recipe steps and then provide the EFT sheet for this section at the end of this appendix.

1. Select an issue to work on. For example, the sharp pain in your lower back. For best results, be as specific as possible about what you are experiencing.
2. Describe the issue. Take a "body scan" of your body to identify where you hold that issue and/or the feeling connected to it. It may be helpful to write down some descriptive adjectives. For example: *tightness, tingling sensation, painful, achy.*
3. Rate it. Rate the level of pain on a scale of zero to ten, with zero being no pain and ten being the worst pain of your life. What's your rating? Write the number down so you remember it.
4. Create the Setup Statement
    It goes like this:
    "Even though _____, I deeply and completely love and accept myself."

Fill in the blank with the issue you identified earlier.

For example: "Even though I have *this sharp pain in my lower back*, I deeply and completely love and accept myself."

5. Begin with the karate chop (KC): With three or four fingers on one hand, tap on the "karate chop" point, found on the little finger side of the hand. It is called this because it is the place on your hand you would hit if you did a karate chop. The points are located on both sides of your body, so it does not matter which side you use. Some people like to tap on both sides simultaneously. You are okay either way you choose. EFT is very forgiving in that way.

You only need to tap each point about seven times, but you don't need to count because you are saying a phrase that will be approximately the same length. If you tap rapidly while saying the phrase, you will have completed the necessary taps.

Tap seven times or more while repeating the setup phrase three times. For example: "Even though I have *this sharp pain in my lower back*, I deeply and completely love and accept myself." Repeat this phase two more times.

6. Head (H): Place the palm of your hand on top of your head (as if you were trying to balance a book on your head). Tap on the crown of your head about seven times or more while saying the following phrase: "This sharp pain in my lower back."

7. Eyebrow (EB): Use two fingers to tap on the spot where one of your eyebrows starts, next to your nose. Tap about seven while saying the following phrase: "This sharp pain in my lower back."

8. Side of Eye (SE): Use two fingers to tap just outside of your eye (not on your temple, and not on the rim of the bone). Tap seven or more times while saying the following phrase: "This sharp pain in my lower back."

9. Under Eye (UE): Use two fingers to tap just under your eye. Tap seven or more times while saying the following phrase: "This sharp pain in my lower back."

10. Under Nose (UN): Use two fingers to tap just under your nose, right in the little groove. Tap seven or more times while saying the following phrase: "This sharp pain in my lower back."

11. Chin (CH): Use two fingers to tap on your chin—not on the chin bone but right in the middle, between your lips and chin. Tap seven or more times while saying the following phrase: "This sharp pain in my lower back."

12. Collarbone (CB): This can be done several ways. I prefer to turn my hand into a fist and then tap on the collarbone spot, which is located about an inch below and about an inch from the middle on the collarbone. Tap seven or more times while saying the following phrase: "This sharp pain in my lower back."

13. Under Arm (UA): Use four fingers to tap on the under-arm spot, which is located at the side of your body, about four inches below your armpit. For women, it is about where your bra lies. Tap seven or more times while saying the following phrase: "This sharp pain in my lower back."

14. 9 Gamat: Turn your hand to face the floor, and locate the spot between your pinky finger and your ring finger (on either hand) in the middle area. Tap on that spot, simultaneously doing the following:

- Eyes closed (just a few seconds)
- Eyes open
- Look down hard right without moving your head
- Look down hard left without moving your head
- Move your eyes clockwise in a circular motion
- Move your eyes counterclockwise in a circular motion
- Hum five seconds of "Twinkle Twinkle Little Star"
- Count to five out loud
- Hum five seconds of "Twinkle Twinkle Little Star"

   I know this sounds ridiculous! What does this do? These exercises are called bilateral brain stimulation, designed to stimulate the left and right brain hemispheres. This stimulation assists the brain to process stored emotions related to traumatic events, both big and small.

15. Reassess the pain intensity level: Reassess the pain level of the memory/emotional pain on a scale of zero to ten. It should drop down the scale by one to three points. It may come down even more, depending on the person and circumstance.

16. Perform another EFT Basic Recipe until the number you started with is down to zero.

Each chapter offers a specially designed script for the various topics discussed. Return to each chapter and find your script; then tap into your amazingness! I believe in you! You got this!

$\mathcal{A}$ppendix C

To Eliminate Self-Sabotage
https://vimeo.com/talkingwithteri/sabotage

Please check out our video for the proper hand placement.

1. Tap side of hand fifteen times (on the karate chop point).
2. Bring right hand to collarbone (with thumb and first two fingers) and rub. Place left index finger in belly button. Rub for a few seconds.
3. Bring left hand to collar bone (with thumb and first two fingers) and rub. Place right index finger in belly button. Rub for a few seconds.
4. Tap under nose fifty times (using first finger and middle finger to stimulate that point).
5. Tap under lower lip fifty times (using first finger and middle finger to stimulate that point).

$\mathscr{A}$ppendix D

Daily Intentions Planner Instructions

This is a tool designed to give you more clarity, organization, and structure to help you create your extraordinary life day by day. To order your own copy go to www.talkingwithteri.com.

Disclaimer: Because I tend to follow some of the laws of the universe, this *will* have that feel to it.

I fill out steps 1 through 3 at the very end of my day, right before I go to bed. Why? Research finds that we process information during the last forty-five minutes of the day seven times more than the rest of the information from the day. Try this. Because the brain is already fast at work trying to figure out how it will all get done, see how *easy* filling out your map becomes!

Here are the steps I take and how I fill them in.

Step 1: Universe
This is your big target in life, the goal you are putting out to the universe to work on. You may not be sure *how* it is going to happen, but it will. I recommend no more

than three targets; otherwise you may feel overwhelmed. Because these will stay the same for a while, I type mine in.

Me: What small steps can I take today to get me closer to my big target?

Step 2: Reward
How do I plan to reward myself for being amazing today? The reward itself can be done first thing in the morning if you like; it does not have to be done after you finish everything. You are a ten *all* the time! So celebrate it!

Example: Rewards I have used in the past include having a cup of tea on my back porch after the workday, a treat at Starbucks, extra time at lunch to take a walk around the water fountain. Rewards do not need to cost anything at all. Identify a way to treat yourself to something you enjoy. Get creative, and have fun!

Step 3: Mind Map
I start with the date in the middle and then map out the things that are a priority to do *today*. Do *not* overbook yourself. You want to push yourself but at the same time accomplish your targets. You will build trust with your subconscious self.

Intentions: What are my intentions for the day? What do I desire to see, hear, feel today?
Examples: I am easily and effortlessly checking in with my mind/body/spirit. I am asking my expansive questions today. I am seeing some sort of symbol today (be specific about what that is. This helps to the strengthen the muscle of the RAS in the brain.) For example, one day I said I need to see a sign of hope; the very next day I went downstairs to see that the television was on at seven (we never have

it on in the morning—never!). As I turned the corner I heard, "If you build it they will come." Chills consumed my body. I just knew what that meant for me. I sometimes simply draw a shape I desire to see sometime during the day: for example, the shape of a heart. When I say it, and I always do, it just provides the evidence of how magical I am as a being, able to bring that into my awareness.

Being: How do I want to show up?
Examples: Playful, grateful, happy, free, energetic, with a giving mentality, mindful, calm, patient, etc.

At the end of the day I return to fill out steps 4 and 5.

Step 4: Evidence of Movement
What have you seen, heard, or experienced that shows you there has been movement toward your target?

Examples: Perfect new client called today; call from a local news station; a sign of hope ("if you build it, they will come"); received great feedback from a friend, etc. This can be small or large, but this will support and build evidence so you see your progress.

Step 5: Gratitude
What am I grateful for today?
Examples: My husband; special playtime with my daughter; my amazing friends; tried new and delicious food; it's Saturday and I relaxed today; the walk around the park with my dog; great connection with my neighbor I haven't seen in a while, etc. You don't need to limit yourself here. Think of as many as you can—the more the better.

Then I create a new one for the next day. Go create and have *fun*!

Universe

✶ ───────────────────────────────

✶ ───────────────────────────────

REWARD: ───────────────────────

Me

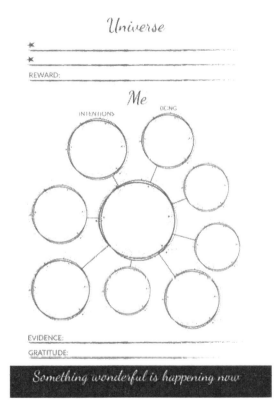

INTENTIONS

DOING

EVIDENCE: ──────────────────────

GRATITUDE: ─────────────────────

Something wonderful is happening now

$\mathcal{A}$ppendix E

How To Pull It All Together To Make the Most Out of Your Day

First forty-five minutes of the day:
Meditation
Exercise EFT (Identify areas that are holding you back and use this tool to eliminate it!)
Energy questions (multiple times throughout the day)
Self-Sabotage Exercise (at least ten times a day)
Drive to work listening to inspirational/education audiobooks
Throughout the day: finding things to be grateful for, asking energy questions, using the very tools taught in this book. I use the clearing statement to clear out anything that shows up that blocks me.

Last forty-five minutes of the day:
Fill out my daily intentions planner
Gratitude journal

Unlock and Embrace Your *Extraordinary!* Questionnaire

Date_____

Own Your Happiness (one, highly disagree; five, highly agree)

I make it a priority to take care of myself and my needs.	
I take full responsibility for my actions, behaviors, and thoughts.	
The glass is half full versus half empty.	
I make choices in my life that are congruent with my desires.	
Total:	/20

Create Your *Rockstar* Team (one, highly disagree; tive, highly agree)

I have a significant number of people who are my personal cheerleaders and seek to see me succeed.	
I am satisfied with the level of support from my friends, family, and colleagues.	
My support team challenges me for the benefit of my personal growth.	
I easily ask for support when I need it.	
Total:	/20

Eliminate Your Head Trash (one, highly disagree; five, highly agree)

I have a belief system that is filled with confidence, competence, and inner knowingness.	
I have worked on my "old stories," and they are no longer a part of my new success story.	
I seek out resources to eliminate my head trash to allow myself to step into my amazingness.	
I use words to build myself up instead of tear myself down.	
Total:	/20

Play Outside Your Comfort Zone (one, highly disagree; five, highly agree)

I often seek out new experiences and adventures that push me to expand.	
I am committed to allowing my life to unfold and being open to all the possibilities that life brings.	
I engage in continual daily personal growth.	
I am a risk-taker.	
Total:	/20

Be Grateful (one, highly disagree; five, highly agree)

I often share with others how grateful I am to have them in my life.	
I can easily find the gifts in any situation (positive or negative).	
I write and send thank you cards on a regular basis.	
I easily find things to be grateful for each day.	
Total:	/20

Celebrate (one, highly disagree; five, highly agree)

I love my life! I have so much to celebrate!	
I celebrate my successes and failures, for each one takes me one step closer to the life of my dreams.	
I find fun ways to celebrate me being a ten every day!	
I celebrate the successes of those around me, as it is more evidence that people can create anything they desire.	
Total:	/20

Take Inspired Action (one, highly disagree; five, highly agree)

I am clear on my life's purpose, and I take steps every day to create more of what I desire in my life.	
I have written down my goals/targets for the year, and I have exceptional follow-through.	
I have an accountability partner to help me achieve my goals/targets.	
I utilize my support team to achieve my goals/targets.	
Total:	/20

Scoring:

0–79. Thank you for being courageous and honest with yourself. You may have found yourself stuck in the muck. You may have realized that you are not fully in love with where you are in life. Some days may feel heavy, when you don't feel like you have much to be grateful for. You are on the right track. You've picked up this book or have been given this book for a reason. Embrace this in your life, and let's start creating the life of your dreams. I give you permission to step out of mediocrity and to be open to all your amazing possibilities! You deserve this!

80–99. You may have seen better times in your life and wonder how you have ended up here. You show signs that you are on the right path and stepping back on the path of your amazingness. You will discover tools to keep you free of your own self-sabotage and launch you toward your own greatness, but you already knew that! I give you permission to continue taking one step at a time. Be your amazing!

100–119. You are well on your way to discovering your true amazingness! You have identified your areas of strength and areas where you can continue to improve. You will find some great tools within this book to launch you into your full potential! I give you permission to be open to discovering how amazing you are so you can help others do the same! You are fabulous!

120–140. You *rock*! You are living your life to the fullest! You have mastered the seven areas in your life and love it! This book will serve as a reminder. It may give you some new tools that will keep you living extraordinary! I give you permission to join the movement toward inspiring and empowering others on your path to be their own greatest gift to this world! Continue to live your life to the fullest!

CPSIA information can be obtained
at www.ICGtesting.com
Printed in the USA
FFOW03n2148130218
45059925-45469FF